I AM A PART OF ALL
THAT I HAVE MET

Clayton Chris Sutter (1919-)

as told to

Rachel Kreider (1909-)

written in Goshen, Indiana, 2010-11

Cover design: rug woven by Clayton C. Sutter, ca. 2000

ISBN-13: 978-1482746037

Goshen, Indiana: CreateSpace, 2013

Greencroft, Valentine's Day, 2009

FOREWORD

In the summer of 2011 my father handed me a 128-page typescript memoir, a collaboration with his friend and neighbor Rachel Kreider. In many conversations with her over the course of a year and a half he had reminisced about his life. She would pose leading and follow-up questions and take notes, then return to her apartment to type them up. Reading these back to him naturally prompted further recollections, editing and corrections.

Physically the document resembles a quilt or comforter. Rachel stapled typed strips of paper with corrections and addenda onto the fronts and backs of the pages. She added small corrections and instructions—"over, for insert"—in a small, fine hand like embroidery. And when needed she carefully applied Wite-Out correction fluid, a product that will seem as foreign to late 21st-century readers of this book as the husking peg does to its 2013 readers.

In content the memoir is more like the rag rugs that my father took such pleasure in creating. It weaves together many fragments—some colorful, others drab—into a long, coherent story. As I read it for the first time I admired its remarkable descriptive detail (for example, the extensive accounts of Midwestern farm life in the 1920s and 30s), its candor, and its flashes of wit.

When he entrusted me with his memoir my father asked me to "type it in the computer," edit it, and prepare it for distribution to family, friends, and other interested readers. To do so has been an honor and a pleasure.

Sem Christian Sutter
Washington, DC
New Year's Day, 2013

HOW DEAR TO MY HEART ARE THE SCENES OF MY CHILDHOOD

I was born on October 17, 1919, on a rental farm located midway between Hopedale and Minier, Illinois. Our family doctor was either Dr. Rost or Dr. Holmes. They were the doctors in these towns but I don't know who had which office. I only know that the one who was ours called upon the other one for consultation and assistance when they saw that my mother was going to have a very difficult delivery. She was a rather small woman and her babies—nine of them ahead of me—usually weighed eight or nine pounds. Even the two doctors felt it necessary to call in a specialist from Bloomington and at one point my father fainted.

All this must have required some time while my mother was suffering, but eventually I, a twelve-pound son, made my appearance. I had trouble breathing and it was serious enough that two of the doctors gave up on me. "There's no use wasting time on him," they declared, but our family doctor did not agree. "You two take care of the mother," he said, "I'll not give up on the boy." Mother and son came through the ordeal, but it was particularly hard for my mother because she was still feeling the effects of an accident that had happened two months before and was especially grieving for her sister Nellie who had lost her life in that accident.

My mother was the second of eight Miller daughters and Nellie was the youngest. She was married to Chris Nafziger and they had three little children—Carroll, Victor, and Bernice. That family and my parents went to visit sister Alice, who had married Dan Stalter, and they lived about forty miles away. On their way home the car lights went out, which happened quite often in those days. They thought they had fixed the lights, but after a second failure they stopped in Bloomington for help. It was late enough that the business places had already closed. They could, however, buy a good flashlight which they hoped could help them get home safely through the remaining miles. Nellie held the

1

flashlight while Chris did the driving. The lights from an approaching car so completely blinded him that there was a collision. The windshield shattered and the flying glass cut Nellie's throat. I don't remember how they said they got Nellie to the hospital, but she soon bled to death there with her family, including my mother, around her. The two youngest children immediately came into the care of our family and therefore they were with my sisters in the big bedroom two months later when I was struggling to make an appearance.

My mother apparently went into post-partum depression. I don't know how long it lasted, but it was very hard on her, especially because of her grieving for Nellie. Once when she was rocking me and nothing seemed to stop my crying, she decided to try singing. When she saw her daughters reacted in joyful surprise, she realized how her mood had affected them. "I must snap out of this," she said to herself. "It is not fair to the other children."

After that she sang often as she rocked me — rocked and sang until I was old enough to remember some of the songs. One of them was:

> Baby bye, here's a fly.
> Come, let's watch him, you and I--
> How he crawls up the walls,
> Yet he never falls.
>
> If you and I had two such legs,
> You and I could walk on eggs.
> Here he is! There he goes!
> Tickling, tickling Baby's nose!

Another one was:

> Twenty froggies went to school
> Down beside the rushing pool.
> Twenty coats of sobering green,
> Twenty vests all white and clean.
>
> We must be on time, said they.
> First we study, then we play.
> That is how we keep the rule
> When we froggies go to school.

Twenty froggies grew up fast.
Lessons they had learned at last.
Now they sit at other pools
Teaching other little fools.

A more serious one included the words:

You are starting, my boy, on life's journey
Along the great highway of life.
You'll meet with a thousand temptations:
The cities with evil are rife.

The refrain to each verse was:

Have courage, my boy, to say NO!
Have courage! Have courage!
Have courage, my boy, to say NO!

I had a very good relationship with my parents. The people that I knew called them Chris and Dellie. Formally they were Christian Sylvester Sutter and Idella Mae (Miller) Sutter, but they were Papa and Mama to me and—along with my sisters—were the heart of my world. My sisters said I wasn't spoiled, but I'll admit that years later, out in the cold world, I found that not everybody would treat me the way my family did.

I enjoyed unlacing Papa's shoes when he would be reading the newspaper. At noon when he would be taking a rest before heading out into the fields again I liked to put on his hat and walk about. When he roused and was ready to leave he would say, "Where's my boy? If I can find my boy, I can find my hat." Since heavy farm work was exhausting, he often went to bed early. I liked to crawl into bed beside him half dressed, begging him to tell me stories about when he was a little boy. I especially cherished this time with him and some of these stories stayed in my memory for years. Long afterward, when Greencroft retirement community asked each of us to make or produce something from our past, I put together for the exhibit a little booklet of stories that I still remembered. On the front cover is a picture of Papa and me. I was standing beside him on my little wagon.

Clayton and Papa, ca. 1921

One of my earliest memories is of gathering nuts. We had a rather large plot of timber on our farm that contained many walnut and hickory trees. The family would go to the woods in the farm wagon, would pick up the nuts that had fallen to the ground, and then empty the buckets into the wagon. The noise of that process and the jerking of the wagon as we went over the uneven ground was very frightening to me. My mother would try to comfort me by saying, "See! Mama is here and so is Papa. Your sisters are here and they are not afraid. You don't need to be afraid either," but I could not be comforted.

Often on winter evenings Papa would sit on the floor behind the living room stove to crack nuts. He had a wooden block that had a hollowed-out place where he put a nut. He then would crack it open with a hammer. We would laboriously pick out the nut meats and put them into a coffee cup. Mama would store the nuts to use later in a variety of ways. What I liked best was to nibble as we went along until Papa would stop me with, "Now you've had enough—or you'll get sick."

I enjoyed standing on a chair beside the kitchen table to watch Mama do the baking. As she kneaded the bread she would give me a little dough to work on. It was a real satisfaction to make my own special bread and to eat it while it was still warm. I also liked to watch Mama roll out the dough into large thin circles for pies. She would often put jelly on a little piece and roll it up or put cinnamon and sugar on scraps of dough and bake them with the pies. When Mary, the sister just older than I, was in school I could have these treats all to myself. I found it so interesting to watch Mama cut up a chicken. After the feathers had been picked off, she would go to the stove with the chicken in one hand and a paper in the other. Lighting the paper, she would waft it over the chicken to singe off all the hairs and pin feathers. Then she would begin to cut up the chicken and I would watch for the heart and gizzard. (I hadn't seen gizzards for many years and then one day I spied a packet of gizzards in Everett's grocery store. I had to buy them for old times' sake.) Mama would pull the skin off the chicken feet and if they were very young she would fry them and serve them with the usual platter. If they had developed very much she boiled the feet and I could gnaw what little meat there was in the padding on the bottom or along the bones.

During corn-husking time Papa often hired help. When the weather was not favorable for field work, the men would go hunting. Then we could have rabbit or squirrel meat for variety and occasionally even pheasant. Sometimes Papa climbed up in the barn to get young squabs; the pigeons were too old.

We ate together as a family three times a day. We always had a tablecloth instead of oilcloth and Mama would put paper under and around my plate. I was still sitting in the high chair but the tray had been removed. Our breakfasts were substantial. In the winter we often had liverwurst on fried potatoes. I was seldom on hand for the breakfasts in those days. I would usually go to bed when Mama did. After Papa's stories I usually went to sleep and she would carry me to my own bed. In the mornings I would come to breakfast after I was "slept out" and the others had already finished theirs. Then I could have what Mama had kept warm for me. I liked to see the thin little scum that had formed on my cocoa cup.

I also liked to stand on a chair by the high kitchen window to see what was going on the other side of the road. Our house and buggy shed were on one side of the road and the barn and outbuildings on the other side. I was not allowed to cross the road and I could not see what Papa was doing during his chores in the barn. I remember seeing Eli "breaking in" the horses. He was my sister Fannie's husband and came from Nebraska. He was interested in horses and I remember how he worked with a team that was not yet trained and wanted to run away. When they would start, Eli would pull on the hobbles, bringing them to their knees. When they were released and started to run again, Eli would repeat the process.

I also remember watching the cattle grazing on that side of the road. I particularly remember a white steer that stood out in the herd in that field. I knew enough about butchering beef for meat that I was not upset when I saw that white steer's head in a pan in our kitchen, but I was awed when I detected some quivering going on.

When Fannie and Eli were still living in town I remember that Mama left me there with Fannie one day when she must have been on some errand. They had hired a man to plow their garden and it happened that he came with his team of horses while I was there. I heard him yell at his horse using the word *son-of-a-gun*. That was a new word for me, but Fannie quickly explained that it was a very bad word and I must never say it. I wondered about this. *Son* was a good word and so was *gun*. I decided it must be that word *of* between them that made the word so bad, but I was puzzled.

We always had a playbox in our house as far back as I can remember. In it were blocks, spools, and a doll with a metal head. I also played with Tinkertoys and clothespins. I could make fences with the clothespins and with Mama's variety of spools I could make them be the animals behind the fences—cows, chickens, or whatever I was imagining at the time. I remember going shopping with Mama and my sister Della one day shortly before Christmas. The stores had so many things to attract my attention, but one thing stood out above the others. I spotted a little train—a little metal red engine with a green passenger car attached. I couldn't admire it long, for I had to keep up with the others. My only brother, the oldest in the family, was already away and had a little family of his own. They were coming home for Christmas and in the rearrangement of beds I got to sleep on the Murphy bed. This had been used only for company and I was delighted to get to use it. To add to my joy and excitement I found the next morning when I woke up — there on my pillow was that little train!

With nieces and nephews so near my age, there was always somebody to play with. We often played house, especially under a fruit tree near the house. I can't remember whether it was a cherry or an apple tree, but I can remember that it was near the chicken house. One day Fannie's daughter Dorine and I were making mud pies under that tree. With the chickens so close it gave me the idea of using eggs in our pies just as real cooks do. We found the eggs so hard to crack. In the effort I got egg yolk all over my fingers and wiped them off as necessary on my overalls. When we were called to dinner Mama looked at the front of those yellowed overalls and wanted an explanation. "We were making mud pies," Dorine explained. I think the family, including Mama, were amused, but she firmly let us know that eggs were not to be played with.

I was only two years old when Fannie married. Now she and her family lived on a farm about a mile away and we were back and forth very often. She knew what a thrill it would be for a little boy to get a present through the mail rather than to have it handed to him. She therefore filled a Whitman candy box with her homemade candy and had the mailman bring it to our box as a birthday present. Indeed it was a thrill. I had never received any mail before and I kept that box for years. It was sturdy enough that it could hold my valuables until I went to high school.

Mama was a very busy woman, but I remember how on winter evenings, when she would be occupied with mending, that she had time to tell us stories. One of them that I remember was an answer to our question as to why the hook on our screen door was placed so high. She said when she was a little girl she and her cousins would cross a nearby creek to play in the sand on the other side. She had received a cup from a special friend. She liked it very much and knew that she was not to take it outside. The temptation was too great for her one time and she took it across the creek. That evening when she was half asleep in bed she remembered that she had left that precious cup in the sand. Sleepily she got up, went out through the screen door and across that log to pick it up. Years later when she thought about the danger she had been in she saw to it that the hook on the screen door was high enough that none of her little children could get out of the house while walking in their sleep.

I liked to hear about the team of white mules she and Papa had once owned. Their names were Bert and Mert. They were ornery in sort of an endearing way. They were determined to go at their own pace and they refused to go faster. But let another team come up even and they began to race. They were not about to let another team get ahead of them. When they heard the band play, their ears would go back and forth in time with the music! They could be so stubborn. Once when several people were trying to get them through a gate they refused to go. They jumped over the fence instead and then stood there and looked back triumphantly as if to say, "We won the game!" We enjoyed the story so much and even Mama laughed until the tears came.

Another story she told was how she had a nightmare and thought her sister Alice was coming after her with a hot stove poker. To protect herself she flung out her arm. It happened that she really did that, swinging it in Papa's direction. He was turned toward her and she really hit his prominent nose very hard. Needless to say by that time they were both awake.

We regularly attended the Mennonite church about six or seven miles away, often riding in the surrey. My family had a car before I was born—a J. I. Case sold by a local farm machine company. That Illinois soil was black and heavy and the roads weren't paved. When it rained the cars could easily get stuck in the mud. Illinois had a poll tax and farmers could get a certain discount if they kept up the road along their property. Thus the care of the roads was uneven. It was also a general practice to oil the roads and if it rained the surface was slick. So much depended on the weather that we used the car mostly in the late spring or early fall. In the winter we usually simply drained the radiator in the car and jacked it up for the winter months and so the surrey was our most frequent mode of transportation to get to church. We all got into one vehicle, whether the car, the surrey, or bobsled. My brother Lawrence had his own car by the time I came along. Perhaps my older sisters may have ridden with him, but I don't recall. When there was enough snow we would ride in the bobsled. Papa would put the wagon box on runners and fill it with fresh straw. Mama and the rest of us would huddle in the straw under a cowhide robe or blankets. Papa stood up to drive, bundled up in a heavy overcoat, ski mask-type cap and big cowhide mittens. The bobsled ride was an adventure that I liked.

Our church was known as the Hopedale Mennonite Church. It was a plain rectangular building with white weatherboard siding. Nearby was a row of white painted sheds with open fronts. The more well-to-do would pay a fee for the use of one and would drive the car or horse into it. There was room only to get in and out of the vehicle. Also there were some hitching posts in the church yard.

The inside was one large room with an aisle down the middle and side aisles along the walls. The wooden benches had straight backs. The women would sit on the left side and the men on the right. I knew that the grandmas sat in the front left-hand corner, facing the pulpit, and the grandpas on the other side. We called those the Amen Corners but no one ever said "amen" except at the end of the prayers.

As long as I was in diapers I sat with my mother. Both my parents would sit in the front third of the church on their respective sides.

The service would be so long and the mothers often gave their little folks crackers from their handbags to help endure the tedium. We did not stand when we sang hymns but we always knelt for prayer, facing the benches. I was surprised and puzzled when during one of those prayer times a grown woman whispered to my mother, asking whether she might have a few of those crackers too.

We had Sunday School first, after we all met together for the opening exercises of songs, scripture, and prayer. As soon as I was old enough I went to the beginners' class which met in an alcove on the main floor. The church had no basement. There must have been about a dozen or so of us in my class and we sat on a bench that had a partition in it. The boys sat on one side of it and the girls on the other. I liked to sit next to that partition, especially since I saw that Marcella Good was trying to get to the other side of it too. We sang the familiar songs like "Jesus Loves Me" and "Jesus Wants Me for a Sunbeam." Our parents had given each of us a penny for the collection and the teacher would go down the row holding a glass jar with a domed top that had a slit in it. She would tell us a Bible story and give us each a card with a picture on it that illustrated the story. There was printing on the back but of course I paid no attention to that.

By that time I was old enough to sit with Papa. I would get to him before the older children got to their seats. The older boys met in the men's cloakroom, or anteroom, which we called the Kämmerli, [the "little room]. I always watched them file back into the sanctuary with a kind of self-conscious swagger as they walked to their seats toward the front.

The service was so long and uninteresting to me. My sisters had handkerchiefs which they could roll or fold into various objects but I had nothing to occupy me—nothing to do. When I could hardly endure the monotony I would swing my legs quite vigorously until Papa's big hand on my knee would stop the action. I liked to sit near Emanuel "Man" Eash for he would slip me a chocolate-covered peanut. Our three preachers had last names, but to us they were Ben, Simon, and Dan [Springer, Litwiller, and Nafziger]. Ben and Simon would preach in English, but every third Sunday Dan would preach in German. Then the time would really drag out. Dan had a habit of clearing his throat and then adding a German expression that I think meant something like "and so we see that...." To help pass the time I would often take note of how many times he would do that. Sometimes I would spend some time concentrating on the kerosene lamp hanging in a movable bracket up on the wall near me, mentally tracing the outline of the ordinary oil lamp with its wick and glass chimney and the reflector behind it. There were a number of these spaced in the room. I think one reason I could endure these long services that I did not understand was because I knew that it was something that everybody just did.

The German services were appreciated by the older members of the church who spoke German fluently and who still had rather close connections with the Old Country. My own great-grandfather had come from Germany in 1848. His name was Christian Suttor and according to family papers he came from the district of Neuburg, Bavaria, north of Munich. They also indicate that his father was Johann Suttor married to Barbara Oesch. They had ten children and owned a great deal of land. As he inspected his estate he would ride on the back seat of his carriage, drawn by a team of fine black horses driven by one of his hired men.

Forsthof, Suttor farm in Bavaria, Birthplace of Christian Sutter
(photo ca. 1900)

Johann Suttor was also a minister in the Amish Mennonite Church and therefore was opposed to warfare and militarism. Germany had a system of military training that in Christian's time required every young man to take two years of training and then for a certain number of years he was to return to camp annually for a time unless he hired a substitute to take his place. Christian had a little of the training, but with the family and church opposed to military service it was decided that he should go to America. There is no evidence that he ever had permission to leave the country, but it is not clear how he was able to escape as a fugitive.

After landing in America he made his way to Tazewell County, Illinois, where others from the old community had rather recently settled. For a year he worked for a farmer. By that time he was ready to begin farming on his own and he married Magdalena Nafziger. They started out under rather difficult pioneer circumstances, getting along as best they could. Unused to such primitive conditions, he became homesick for his old life and family. He sent glowing reports to those he had left behind about possibilities in Illinois, encouraging them to come to America.

They for their part were ready to leave Germany. His brother Joseph was serving in the army and there were three more coming along who would have to face the military. A year later the family too made the difficult journey to America. When they finally arrived and saw what pioneer life in Illinois was like they were disappointed and even upset. The brothers were so angry that they decided to give Christian a beating. When they came to the house to take their revenge, they found that Magdalena had locked them out until their tempers could cool down.

At first the farmers found the wet and uneven heavy soil not very good for farming, but Christian was among those who dug ditches to drain the land and soon they found out how fertile the soil really was. Christian, an ambitious entrepreneur, kept adding acreage until he eventually owned considerable land in central Illinois. He was progressive and prosperous. When farmers planted their corn, they could set their planters to drop the seed at regular spaces. Christian became so expert that he could set the planter to space uniformly that later the cultivator could go through the rows either way to root out the weeds. At harvest time he was able to buy up other people's corn and hold it for more favorable prices. It was therefore his responsibility to get the grain across the Mackinaw River to Pekin. This sometimes meant blazing a trail through the area and fording the stream. One time a sudden swirl in the current lifted the wagon box and it started going downstream. Fortunately it did not go far and could be rescued.

It is not surprising that Christian was the first one in the church to put a top on his buggy (and I suppose there were side curtains to attach in bad weather). The rowdy young boys threw stones at the buggy, whose top their elders probably — out of conviction or envy — considered a sign of pride.

He also built the historic Sutter barn in 1868. He wanted to build a barn big enough to hold church services, and that is how it came to pass that an important conference was held there in 1875 when the Amish Mennonites of Illinois decided how they wanted to be affiliated. This gave it historical significance among Mennonites. When the Sutter estate was settled the farm on which the barn was located went to daughter Magdalena Hieser. In the 1970s after the Illinois Mennonite Heritage Center was established at Metamora, descendants in the family donated the barn to the museum. It was taken down, restored, and put up on the museum grounds. Another Illinois family, the Schertzes, donated a little country house to go with it and it now holds my parents' bedroom furniture which my sister Carrie gave to the museum.

Christian and his wife Magdalena had four children: Barbara,

Christian, John, and Magdalena. After his wife's death he married a Mrs. Augsburger who had children of her own. When his large estate was eventually settled after his death in 1899 she contested the terms of the will, despite a property agreement after their marriage. She was so aggressive and demanding that her children get shares that hard feelings developed. The case went all the way to the Illinois Supreme Court which ruled against her. Son Christian, my grandfather, did inherit a farm.

He had married Fannie Stalter and they did not move to the farm immediately. Years before then Grandpa had suffered through such a severe case of measles that he was weakened for life and was not strong enough to handle heavy farm work. They had thirteen children, nine of them sons. As the older boys grew strong enough to help, the family moved to the farm, where the children grew up. All of them except two eventually settled in the local area. Uncle Aaron and Uncle Cyrenius married girls from Iowa and raised their families there.

Papa was the oldest in that family and of course was named Christian too. However, when he had a son he said there were enough Christian Sutters and he named my brother Lawrence. By the time I came along—after Fannie, Della, Marie (who died as an infant), Carrie, Bessie, Lydia, Minnie, and Mary—they were willing to name me Clayton Chris, so the name continued in a different form.

Grandpa Sutter was a tall man, over six feet, and his nickname was Shorty. I remember his white hair, his bent-over torso, and his little white beard (chin-whiskers!). I remember less about Grandma. Perhaps we spoke less to each other because of her German and it may have been a small difference, but she had so many little ones around her and she received me with the same smiles and cookies as all the rest.

When Grandpa was still active enough, butchering days were at their house and some neighbors and family members would join in. One story has been told about the argument Grandpa and Grandma had about how much pepper to put into the sausage. He wanted about twice as much as she did. He had strong opinions and won the argument. People who came in to help on butchering days could always take some meat along home. When our family tried the sausage later at home they found it so impossibly peppery that they threw it out. "Even old Spot won't eat it!" exclaimed Mama.

Spot, a white dog with black spots, had been in our family for years. He was like a member of the family. He seemed to think he was too when he jumped up for the jelly bread I had been eating outdoors. He was a farm dog and did not come into the house. One morning he came home so bruised and scratched that Papa said he must have been fighting a coon. So fearful were my parents of rabies that they declared he had to be put to sleep. I was persuaded to agree and thus took his death in stride, as I did so many other things.

By the time I really knew Grandpa Sutters they had already left the farm, renting it to Uncle Amos, and they were living in retirement in Hopedale. When we would visit them I was impressed with their electricity and indoor plumbing. They had a cement driveway all around the house. What fascinated me most was the dumb waiter inside. I wanted to be on hand when Aunt Tillie would mysteriously pull those little shelves up from the cellar and then send them down again with the butter and other dishes of food that were to be kept cool.

Grandpa's clan would have a reunion every summer. I especially remember one reunion when we kids had so much fun with Uncle Harvey on the porch swing. He sat in the middle with us crowded around him. With those long legs he could really give us an exciting ride on that swing. We had a wonderful time. He was one of the younger uncles and was still living at home. We appreciated the attention he gave us youngsters. Sometimes he would come out to the farm to play checkers with Papa. Then Mama would make popcorn and we would have a cozy evening.

These Illinois families were my father's people. We all lived pretty much the same way and our church services were very similar. I remember when I first discovered that church services could be quite different and that our neighbors were not all Mennonite. We had a neighbor, Dick Hainline, who was a heavy drinker. One night we heard a shot. Papa said, "Somebody got a rabbit." But it turned out that Dick had climbed a brush pile and took his own life. This is how it happened that we attended a funeral in the Lutheran church. The officiating minister wore a long black robe. In astonishment I whispered, "Mama! That man is wearing a dress!"

I remember another neighbor family who had the same last name but they may not have been related. Mrs. Hainline was an invalid. She had fallen out of a cherry tree and broke her back. When we knew her she was in bed most of the time, but occasionally sat in a wheelchair. Mama would go regularly to see her and did neighborly things. Ray Hainline played the violin and sometimes brought it along to our house evenings. He not only played the violin but could sing and dance. When he would forget the words of a song he might substitute words like "alfalfa hay" over and over until he could remember the words. When he danced a jig Mama said he could shake the whole house. In those days before radio or television he was welcome entertainment.

I was introduced to school when I was five years old, but I had a special experience there before then. The community was included when the school had their Christmas program. Along with the usual pupil performances there would be a Christmas tree with real candles burning in the branches and a Santa Claus to pass out treats. Even the preschoolers in the neighborhood could get their share. As a toddler I went forward to get my bag of candy, but Santa had turned his back. When I put my hand on his leg, he whirled around, so close to the tree that he threatened to topple it. In grasping the tree his cotton beard caught fire and immediately his costume was burning. The fire was put out very quickly and I suppose I got my candy, but I doubt whether I would remember the incident had I not heard the story told and retold.

The teacher in our little country school thought it was a good idea to have those youngsters who would be in the first grade in the fall attend school a few weeks in the spring in order to show them what to expect. Therefore in the spring of 1924 I went to school with my sister Bessie who was in the eighth grade. She packed my lunch with hers and so I got to eat with the older girls. When weather permitted they liked to eat out on the big rocks and I enjoyed listening to their conversations. Living with so many sisters I could feel comfortable in a world of women. With that introduction and the security of going to school with my sisters, I looked forward to becoming a first-grader.

The Burt School was one and a quarter miles away via the road— we never cut across the fields. We walked that distance every day unless it was too rainy or wintry. Then Papa would take us in the surrey or bobsled. If it was bitter cold we stayed at home. As we walked down the road we would soon be joined by three or four of the Williams kids and later on by Grace and Lyle Pratt. Since our school had only about twenty-five pupils our bunch made quite a difference in attendance.

Our school building was a plain white little structure out by itself in the open prairie with no trees around it. It did have some play equipment on the grounds—some swings, a slide, and a teeter-totter. The inside had the usual stove and up front the blackboards, the teacher's desk, and nearby the recitation bench. As usual, the smaller desks were at the front and they gradually became larger as one moved toward the back. There were hooks on the back walls for our wraps. I don't remember where we put our dinner pails, whether on the floor or shelves. They were small, round, metal pails with flat lids and thin, wire-like handles across the top. There was also a bucket and dipper at the back, and we each had a little collapsible drinking cup that we kept at our desks. The teacher had a small brass bell on her desk which she would carry to the door every morning and after each recess to let us know it was time for school to begin.

I don't really remember much about those few months in the first grade at the Burt School. The days were quite ordinary—no fights or excitement. I have only a blur in my memory as to what we were to learn or how we went about it. The teacher would call the classes in turn to come forward to the recitation bench to recite or be tested in their lessons in the short time given to each class. Once when our class was called forward while we were learning to count the teacher asked me how many were in my class. I looked at my half dozen classmates and answered, "A whole bench full."

I remember a few lines of a little poem that has stuck in my mind from those days:

> I saw a little birdie come hop, hop, hop.
> I said to the birdie "Stop! Stop! Stop!"
> He cocked his little head and wagged his little tail...

All I can remember after that is that "the birdie flew far away!"

I missed quite a bit of school in those months because of scarlatina and whooping cough, which had been "going around." I remember that we practiced for the usual Christmas program, but as the year 1924 came to an end something else was claiming my attention more than school — we were going to move to Indiana!

Usually the landowners made arrangements for the coming year in the fall. This year our landlord still had not said anything about it. By the end of the year Papa went to investigate and found that the farm had already been rented to someone else. A neighbor had initiated such favorable proposals that he had yielded but did not inform Papa of what he had done. Now we had to find another place to live and rental properties were very hard to find at that time of year. There simply were none available in our area. As word spread among the relatives about our predicament we heard from Uncle John Reinhardt, married to Mama's sister Lizzie, that there was a farm not spoken for in their community near Kouts in Porter County, Indiana. I never knew how thoroughly my parents investigated it, but at any rate they had no choice. We had to move and move promptly to get the necessary spring work done in preparation for getting the crops planted.

Suddenly a great deal was going on all at once in our family. Mama began packing dishes and glass jars of canned goods into barrels with oats poured around them for protection. Papa rented a box car that would come to the Sutter Siding, a spur of the railroad at my great-grandfather's grain elevator near Hopedale, to load the farm animals we would take along as well as farm equipment and our furniture. Lawrence and Bill Litwiller, Della's husband, would travel in the boxcar to water and feed the animals. A moving date was set for as early in January as we could manage and we younger children were to go to Grandpa

Sutters a few days before that to get out of the way of the last bustle.

The morning of the move was bitter cold. Uncle Elmer was to bring our car to the boxcar and Grandpas to gather us up for an early start. We waited and waited but he did not come. From then on everything that could go wrong did! Because it was so very cold the radiator froze and the car got hot. Uncle Elmer raised the engine hood, which in those days could be lifted off. The hood slipped out of his hand and hit the fan which broke. Since the engine was running, the broken piece went through the radiator and let out all the water. Somehow the men got the car to Uncle Ed's garage. As the car was a 1913 model, he couldn't replace any of the parts. There was nothing to do but try to solder the radiator as best he could. Now, instead of an early morning start, we were beginning our six or seven-hour journey to Indiana after the noon meal. Aunt Alice and Uncle Dan Stalter lived about forty miles away along our route and we therefore stayed there that night.

Our trip the next day was slowed down because we had to stop so often for water for the radiator. They had stuffed rags into the radiator to help retain the water but it was not very satisfactory. On top of that trouble we had two flat tires. Papa got out each time to jack up the car and patch the inner tubes while the rest of us huddled together in the car to keep warm. We of course had no heater in the car but we did have the side-curtains attached. But as my sister said, they were not "draft-free"! Finally, as it was getting dark we had our third flat tire in the vicinity of Kankakee, still on the Illinois side of the state line. By then Papa had used up all his patching materials. Up the road we could see a light. Papa decided to risk driving that far on the rim since there was nothing else to do. The wheels were of wood and we had not driven far at all until one of them broke. Now we were really stranded. Papa walked to the farmhouse and explained the situation. The farmer came with his team of horses and pulled us into their barnyard. They invited us into the house to get warm. Papa phoned Uncle John, who promptly started out to get us, but since we were over fifty miles away we of course didn't get to bed at their house until the wee hours of the morning.

The next day Papa and Uncle John went to buy a new wheel and to bring the car back into use again. Uncle John still had five children at home and it must have been crowded there, but we had to stay there until the boxcar arrived and the furnishings were put into the new place, which was six miles away. Meanwhile I was busy those few days, getting new impressions and new insights. This was the first time I saw oleo, a butter substitute. And it was white! When it was warmed to room temperature yellow coloring could be worked into it until it looked like butter. Otherwise it looked like lard! In the oleo carton were some heavy papers that could be folded according to patterns to make paper furniture. I was fascinated to watch how this could be done. Uncle Johns also had an organ. It was so interesting to see my cousins work the pedals to make the bellows inside make those sounds. I had never seen anything like it. Cousin Mary could play it very well and even little Stella could play a hymn with two fingers that I recognized as "Jesus, Lover of My Soul."

Uncle Johns also had electricity, which came from a Delco plant in the basement. When they were charging the batteries below I could see the brightness changing in the lights that were hanging from the ceiling. The bulbs were covered with simple frosted shades. They also had a pressure tank in the basement. When the flow from the faucets began to weaken someone would go down the stairs to push and pull the long lever back and forth to increase the pressure.

I noticed that we would no longer have to worry about slipping on the roads or get stuck in the mud. The roads were not paved but were covered with crushed limestone, the larger chunks being put down first and then covered with the smaller stones. As the traffic would wear them down the little pebbles would be worked to the sides.

When I got to see our new place I was impressed to see that the house and the farm buildings were all on the same side of the road, this time to the north side. Among them stood a silo and a windmill. I had never seen either one before. An ordinary farm-type wire fence was around the yard and I noticed that a field came right up to it on the left, the west side. I could hardly imagine a cow being able to come that close to our house yard.

The house was shaped like a T, the main part of it having two stories. The kitchen on the left side was set back to form a short base for the T, and it had no upper floor. The front door, one step up and facing the road, led into the dining room. The door to the kitchen also faced the road, but it was set further back and opened onto a little porch. This door was going to be used much more than the "front door." As soon as I stepped inside I could feel how much more space this house was going to give us. A stairway led to the four bedrooms upstairs. The windows were all lower and I could see out so much better. We would be eating in this dining room regularly and so there was going to be a lot of traffic back and forth between the kitchen and the dining room, especially since the dining room also had a door leading to the north—out to the farm buildings and the wash house nearby—and the kitchen did not.

The stoves had been set up and Mama brought a kettle of soup for our first meal there. She built a fire in the kitchen stove, but the smoke would not go up the chimney. No matter what she and Papa tried, an air current kept bringing the smoke back into the kitchen. Mama gave up and pulling aside the domed top to the living room stove she set the soup kettle on the flat surface directly above the fire. Papa, always innovative, went to the tinsmith and had him make a heavy kind of stovepipe that could be inserted in the chimney but reach to the level of the rest of the house. This guided the smoke up the chimney and solved the problem.

With Sunday coming so soon after we settled in, we of course went to the church right away. The Hopewell Church was the only Mennonite church in the settlement. It was five miles away on the outskirts of Kouts, a village of about 600 people. It was located on a corner where two roads intersected and I noticed at once how much more traffic there was around the church. It was a plain stucco building with the front door flush with the walls. There were no sheds or hitching posts. People were coming to church in cars. The few times there was enough snow that we used the bobsled Papa had to tie the horses to the fence.

As we entered the building we went up several steps inside. On the right was the women's cloakroom and the cloakroom for the men on the left, from which stairs led up to the balcony. In the corner of the entryway were steps going down to the basement. The interior of the church was much like that at Hopedale except it was newer and the rounded backs of the factory-made benches were so much more comfortable than the straight-backed homemade ones. Down the middle aisle was a large register, bringing heat from the furnace in the basement. People liked to stand on that register to warm their feet before the service started. Later on I could look down and see that the furnace was red hot. I was told that the trustee's sons were the janitors and if they forgot to give the heating enough time they really fired up the furnace.

After the usual opening exercises we children went to the basement for Sunday School. I wasn't aware of any furnace, for the big room was curtained off to make space for the various classes. There were about eight or nine in our class of first graders, the oldest class to have boys and girls together. Aunt Lizzie Reinhardt was our teacher and we had the same little cards and story time. At the end of class the children were all gathered together for singing and a final word.

When we went upstairs I still sat with Papa. This congregation was smaller and younger. Papa was now considered a grandpa old enough for the amen corner. Sitting a step higher and at right angles to the people I could now rove my eyes over the crowd which was more interesting. I also noticed that in the middle of the windows on each side was a window a little wider than the others and at the top it arched into a kind of peak that I would later think had a kind of gothic effect. It was also new to me to have a woman lead the singing. The preacher was Jacob Birky, the old bishop of the area. His sermon was shorter and he was already showing his age. (He died within the year.)

We also went to school as soon as we could. There the differences were so much greater than between the churches. First of all, we didn't need to walk. The school hack picked us up right in front of our house—Lydia in eighth grade, Minnie in sixth, Mary in third, and I in first. The hack was an elongated buggy with a door at the back and a railing and several steps leading up to it. There were windows and a bench along each side. There was a little stove up front beside the driver. Since it was winter he had pulled down a glass front which, however, gave him enough of a slit underneath for handling the lines (reins) to drive the two horses. The school was only two and a half miles away but until we had made the stops at all the farmhouses we must have driven about ten. Even though it took a long time, it surely beat walking! And I enjoyed the dozen or so pupils in the hack.

The Aylesworth School was "consolidated," located out in the country across from a woods. The playground had no trees or equipment until we later had sold enough Jell-O to bring in a hand-pushed merry-go-round. The building had two main rooms, the one to the left for the first four grades and the one to the right for the other four. Between the rooms was a narrower one, a kind of utility room, used for whatever purposes came up. It held the furnace and when the weather was unfavorable we could eat there and play in the basement. The basement had the basketball hoops—also the toilets with large tanks hanging overhead. There was always a smell of disinfectant.

I had hardly any contact with the pupils or activities of the upper grades. I knew that their teacher was the principal who looked after the furnace and played with his pupils. In our room the first graders' desks were in a row along the windows. The second grade sat in the next row and the fourth grade was farthest from the windows. Those kids would help us first graders with our wraps, especially our boots! There was no recitation bench. When Miss Fisher, our teacher, would call us up front we sat on little oval-backed red chairs around her desk or chair.

In Illinois our schoolbooks were furnished. Here our parents were to supply them. This was impossible for Papa to do and so we had to use stray copies or second-hand or borrowed books. This was not my only handicap. My classmates were doing things and saying things I knew nothing about. It was clear that they had covered many more lessons than I had. I stumbled along in a bewildered sort of way as best I could, but those difficult four months are a kind of blur in my mind. I simply accepted the fact that "this is the way it is" and I said nothing about it to anyone. Miss Fisher was a young teacher. She told us toward the end of the year that she was getting married and wouldn't be back. I suppose she had other things on her mind rather than paying special attention to a little boy that needed help in adjusting. I remember how Miss Fisher would give us each a container of alphabet letters which were to be arranged to look like the words she had put on the blackboard. We had a piano in our room and I liked to hear Miss Fisher play it.

Naturally I liked recess best. We boys were a little too young to use the basketball hoop in the basement but we liked to throw the ball around. A new game I learned was called mumbley-peg. It was played with a jackknife that one of the boys provided. Both blades were drawn out and we took turns tossing the knife with a kind of twirl into the soft ground that was close to the school building wall. The goal was to have the knife land in an upright position and if it was being held up by the small blade the score would be higher than if held by the larger one. If the knife went flat it meant losing a turn. It seems to me we boys mostly just joyfully and energetically "chased around" at recess.

I don't remember any special programs or events until the last day of school when all eight grades had a wiener roast in the woods across the road. The older pupils cut the sticks and it was the first time I held a weenie on a stick over a bonfire. That was fun. But the best of all was that now I could stay home and enjoy the freedom I had been having on weekends. When the first graders ran out of the building and down the walk that last day they held up their report cards and yelled "I passed! I passed!" I was glad that I too had "passed" into the second grade, but I don't recall that I had strong feelings one way or the other. It was much later that I realized Miss Fisher would have done me such a great favor had she held me back another year in order to get a good basic first year of school.

As a third grader my sister Mary was in my room at school and surely knew that I wasn't doing very well, but she never said anything about it that I know of. I'm sure she had her own problems of adjustment but with so many in our family, my siblings were used to looking after themselves. There was a railroad near us that we could not see but we could hear the whistles. One day when Mary heard a whistle, she exclaimed "Oh, Mr. Train Man, take me back to Illinois!" Long afterward I heard that Mama added to herself, "…and take me with you!"

I surely did not realize how discouraged or frustrated my parents must have been that spring, although I remember Mama's calling Uncle John Reinhardt on the phone, asking them, "Can you folks come over for dinner Sunday? Chris is feeling so blue." For one thing it rained and rained that spring, delaying the field work longer and longer. The land was poorly drained and many drainage tiles were broken. The muck land soaked up water like a sponge. When Papa could finally get into the fields, he burned the corn stalks as he had always done before. But the muck started to burn! Papa was not used to muck. He tried to smother it, but it smoldered on and on. I still remember to this day the smell of burning muck. I also remember how one day Papa stood at the window singing "Jesus is All the World to Me," trying to cheer himself up.

Papa went to farm sales to pick up a few things that he needed and could not bring along, but he bought a new binder and new box wagon. The wagons in Illinois had to have thin wheels, for the heavy mud would work its way up on the spokes, but in this Indiana soil the wagon wheels could be much wider. Money was going out for Papa but he was in no position to bring any in. Fortunately, Carrie and Bessie, the oldest sisters that came with us, soon had jobs. Carrie worked for a month or so at a time for families who had new babies and needed extra help. Bessie got a steady housekeeping job with a young family named Marshall who lived in Hebron, about five miles away. Mrs. Marshall was the daughter of the Beekers, our neighbors. This gave us another contact with the neighborhood. Both girls turned their wages back for family use, a real godsend for my parents. I knew we were poor because we were driving an old car when other people had nice sedans!

One of the new experiences for me was Sunday evening church. This was possible because of the electric lights that hung down from the church ceiling. The church could have electricity because they were located at the edge of Kouts. The evening service was called Young People's Meeting. I didn't know that somewhere some people had planned themes for such services, which were announced through the church periodical, along with essay titles and other suggestions for working out an evening program. I knew only that we children were called to the front seats and we in turn would recite a Bible verse. When some of the boys forgot to make any preparation beforehand they could resort to a verse they already knew — "Jesus wept!" We would have a story and some singing and then the program would be turned over to the young people. By then I usually lost interest, although I would take note when my sisters would read their essays.

Later on I also learned that there was another group of Mennonites in our community that had another background and history. We called them the Egli Mennonites because their minister's name was A. D. Egli. They rented the Christian Church building since their congregation was too small to have a building or a full program of their own. Their young people therefore came to our Young People's Meeting and the two groups of young folks met together for the new midweek venture of more secular programs in homes, a project called The Literary. Relationships between the two branches were good and the families would sometimes invite one another to dinner across lines.

By the end of April Papa could get into the field to sow oats and later in May he could plant corn. When serious field work began Carrie would help him in whatever way she was needed. Mama meanwhile put out a garden and gave me a little plot where I planted corn, but I can't remember anything more about it.

Papa suffered from sciatica pain and carried a cane everywhere he went. He had to have his medicine and carried his pills with him. It became a job for Mary and me to bring him — every forenoon and afternoon — the water necessary to swallow those pills. In Illinois I had not been allowed even to cross the road, but now I could walk out across the fields and enjoy the great expanse of Nature. One day we noticed a yellow ball in the distance. In a schoolbook we had seen the picture of a wolf — his color there was yellow. We were afraid and ran to tell Papa that there seemed to be a wolf in the distance, all rolled up in a ball and apparently asleep. Papa went with us to investigate. He explained that it was only an aged puffball, and as he kicked it the dust flew. We had only one cow, but Uncle John had some heifers with her in the pasture and again it was our job to bring those cows to the barn every evening. A whole new world was opening to me as we made those walks across the farm. We had no woods but a tree appeared here and there in a fence row.

Enough rain continued into and through the summer so that the crops rapidly grew lush. So did the weeds. Every two miles or so a ditch had been dredged to help drain the land in our area. One of those crossed our farm. I was alone a lot and that ditch bank was a wonderful place to explore. I watched as the cattails, nettles, and other plants slowly grew higher than my head. On the banks grew pennyroyal, which was good for nibbling and it made such good tea. Sometimes Mama had Mary and me take tea in our water pail to Papa out in the field.

Although I often played alone, I had a new playmate sometimes that summer. My sister Bessie worked for the Marshall family who had a son Jackie that was a little younger than I. Occasionally he came to visit his Grandpa Beekers, our neighbors. Mrs. Beeker would call to see whether I could come over to play with him. I enjoyed those visits. He had some things I never had. One was a cap gun and we played policeman. That would have been an unnatural game at our house. His grandma always gave us treats — Hershey bars, peanuts, or jelly bread. We had to sit on the porch steps as we enjoyed these goodies.

Uncle John's Stella was between Mary and me in age. The cousins soon became best friends. Already in that first summer they began

27

spending a week of each summer in each other's homes. I remember that in the week when Stella was with us we had so much fun in the playhouse that we made in the empty corn crib. Somehow we put the boards together to make a table. Our dishes were mostly can lids — tops that would not seal in canning. For our food we used the red and white blossoms of smartweed and the tiny buttons in mallow weed pods. When we saw how the green thorns on the burdock burrs would stick together we began to make things with them, especially miniature tables and chairs, and what other furniture or objects we could create. It was great fun.

When the Fourth of July came our church and the Egli group had a picnic together. We gathered at a farm home and someone furnished a hay rack where the women could set their well-filled baskets of food. I found out later that the women would vie to see who could have the first fried chicken of the season. Sometimes the bones were quite small! I don't remember just how or where we boys ate, but we enjoyed the eats! Some of the boys had firecrackers to shoot but my parents considered that too dangerous and would not let me have any. However, I watched Papa make a whistle out of a willow switch for me. I could run comfortably with the other fellows, for I had the only whistle and I enjoyed blowing it. After the big meal the young men played the older married men in baseball. The young fellows won, as they usually did. Then came the Big Treat. One of the members worked at the ice cream store. By passing the hat someone got enough money to buy two huge well-packed tubs of ice cream from that store. Ice cream was not new to me but we had it so seldom.

In that summer I went to my first Mennonite funeral. Old Bishop Birky died and he was related to about half the congregation. We sat at a different place from the usual and the front seats were reserved for all the relatives who followed the open casket down the aisle to the front. There were the usual scripture readings, hymns, and sermon. It was a very hot day and the sermon so long that I could hardly endure it. When it was finally over the undertaker directed the people in the back to come down the side aisle, row by row, cross the front past the casket, and then go back to their seats through the other side aisle. The family was thus the last to view the corpse and make their tearful farewells. Then the casket was closed. The pallbearers, who in this case were the bishop's six sons, had been sitting in the amen corner and now along with the minister they preceded the casket down the main aisle to the doors. The mourners followed and then the rest of us. A long line of cars followed the hearse to the graveyard outside of town. I can't remember anything about the committal service but I know the bishop's grave was only the second one in the new Mennonite cemetery. In those days the Mennonite funerals were solemn religious farewells—no flowers or eulogies, but always a reminder that our time was short and we needed to be ready at any time to meet our judgment.

My parents were very hospitable people. Before I was born they even took in members of the extended family if one of them needed a home for an indefinite time. Company was frequent and, though usually unannounced, was seldom a surprise. My family would always rise to the occasion. If families with children stayed overnight, we youngsters would sleep on the floor or make whatever other adjustments were necessary. Relatives on both sides came to visit us in Indiana. Uncle Dan Stalters were among the first. Uncle Dan changed cars about every year and liked to try them out with a trip to Kouts.

When various sets of cousins came to visit Papa brought out his box of the arrowheads he had collected as he cultivated the fields. We were told that many years ago, when Indians roamed this land, that there was a lake on our farm and that the muck and marl was all that was left of it in our day. If Papa dug very deep he would strike marl, a soft whitish limestone that could harden. Sometimes Papa would even find bits of shells in the marl. In the fields it held water and impeded drainage. This old lake also explained the arrowheads. We were told that the Indians would shoot at ducks on the lake.

I knew something about Indians, for the moveable dome top of our living room stove had an Indian in full dress at its peak. Printed at the base was the name CHIEF DOWAGIAC. I knew that Indians by now were people like the big man who delivered ice and our hack driver, Mr. Lightfoot, who was half Indian. Since

Papa had gathered so many arrowheads he would generously offer them to my cousins who happily helped themselves. Perhaps Papa knew that I was uneasy about this, for he strongly assured us that he would be gathering many more. Unfortunately, he never did.

When I played along the ditch bank I saw so many minnows darting about in the water. I also saw some fish that were larger and I told Mama that I would like to go fishing. She helped me fasten a long string to a stick and for carrying it we wrapped the string around and around the stick. At the end of the string she put a bent pin. I found a worm to put on that pin—we could find a pink fish worm any time we wanted one by lifting a board in the walk. Down the road a short distance and over the ditch was a simple wooden bridge with an iron railing, a perfect place to fish—right above the water. Sure enough—before long a small fish had gone after the bait and was hooked! I laboriously rolled the string up around the stick again, rejoicing that the fish stayed attached. I triumphantly carried it home to Mama who cleaned the fish and fried it for my supper. What a thrill!

By August the crops had matured and then came the threshing season. (We said "thrashing.") Someone in the neighborhood owned a thrashing rig which consisted of a steam engine, the machine itself, and the water wagon, which was a huge tank, drawn by a team of horses. When Mary and I would see the outfit coming down our road as it went from farm to farm we would run to the road to watch it pass by. When the driver of the engine was near us he would reach up and pull on the strap to give us a whistle. Then we three would grin as the rig rumbled by.

When it came to our house the so-called "engineer" settled the machine in the pasture by our house yard. I could watch him locate the engine and connect the broad belt between the engine and the threshing machine. The man on the water wagon drove down to the ditch to pump the water needed to make the steam for the engine. Soon two wagon racks of wheat sheaves came from the field where the grain bundles had been piled into shocks for drying. By the time these bundles had been fed into the machine two other wagons of sheaves were on hand to keep the process continuous. With a great deal of noise the machine thrashed the wheat, sending straw through a huge blower to a stack on the ground. The grain meanwhile accumulated in a metal container that when filled to a certain weight would automatically dump the wheat into a box wagon. In this way the yield was measured. When the box was full it was hauled away to the elevator along the railroad. By the time it came back a second box wagon was almost full.

Papa was busy supervising the entire process and deciding how much grain he would keep for seed and how much for feed for the livestock through the winter. The crop was disappointing this year. We had sown the "winter wheat" in the fall and when water stood in hollows so long this year the wheat either froze out or was drowned out. In order to get a crop Papa sowed oats into the low land. When this mixed grain was to be sold at the elevator it of course had to go for a lower price.

The oats thrashing came next. The rains had made the stalks flourish so much that they reached up to Papa's outstretched arms. He had a picture taken of this to show the remarkable growth. When the oat bundles were thrashed, however, a great reddish dust rose, showing that the crop had been infected with rust. The grain was not fully developed and this again affected the price.

Even the corn was disappointing that year. Papa couldn't get it planted until too late to have a long enough season for proper drying in the ear. When the growing season was over Papa and hired help drove into the corn field and with hand husking pegs would remove the husks row by row, tossing the ears into the wagon. This year they had to discard many moldy ears. Papa knew before the corn was cribbed for the winter that it would not get dry enough to command a good price.

I was in school during much of the corn harvest, but I liked very much to be on hand when the corn was put up in the crib. The crib was almost as big as the barn and had a drive-through in it. Papa would store other things in the top when convenient. When a wagon load was drawn up beside the crib it was tipped at an angle so that when the end-gate was removed at the bottom the corn could flow down into a chute connected with a chain belt with cross bars to hold the ears as they were drawn up and then dropped inside. The mechanism controlling the process was in a little wooden structure above the crib that we called the elevator and we used horse power for the operation.

Papa would unhitch the team from the wagon and hitch the horses to a long rod fastened to a large wheel. This wheel was geared into a little wheel that somehow brought the horse power to the chain-belt. The nearer horse had a line fastened to his bit which guided the team in a circle. They were so well trained that they didn't need a driver. Papa, standing at the lower end of the wagon, would start the action with the usual click of his tongue in his cheek. The horses would begin to go round and round while Papa fed and controlled the flow of the corn into the chute. He had time to toss out the moldy ears that came along. As soon as I was old enough, my job was to climb up the upper end of the wagon and see to it that all the corn ears moved on down to the chute. When Papa gave the horses a loud "whoa" the action would stop.

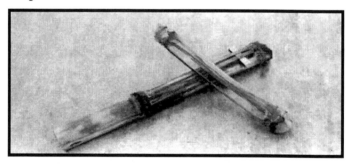

Papa made me a corn stalk fiddle. He picked a healthy corn stalk and cut off the ends beyond two sturdy joints. Then he would make slits on the concave side of the stalk so as to have two "strings" and underneath he would push the pithy part of the stalk toward the ends. Sometimes it took the pith of another stalk to stuff enough in that the strings were taut and raised above the rest of the stalk. Then he would do much the same to another stalk to make the bow, except that he would cut on the rounded part of the stalk and make only one string. When the parts were wet (spitting on them was all that was necessary sometimes) he would draw the bow across the strings and make a sound!

Our family had to bear one more disappointment that fall. When we moved we had brought along seventeen horses but through the summer thirteen of them had gotten sick and died. They were stricken with what was called marsh fever. The Indiana horses seemed to be immune to it. I remember how often Papa would come in from the barn to say that another horse had died in the stall. A team of horses with chains would pull the dead horse out to behind the barn where he laboriously dug a hole big enough to bury it.

On top of all this, Papa was suffering from sciatic pain that often was so severe he could hardly manage. Farmers often had to consider their vocation as a gamble. Like the weather, many things were beyond a farmer's control. My parents could have complained bitterly that fall, or even given up, but I could see then already how they had an unusual ability to endure adversity. They simply said, "Next year we hope will be better."

When I started to school that fall so much seemed like new beginnings. I had a new teacher and there were new kids in my room. We started out with the old school hack, but halfway through the year Mr. Lightfoot got sick and his wife took over. Now a car took us to school, but it had to make several trips to get us all picked up. By the third grade we had a real school bus, a very dark green one. We were proud of that bus. After it dropped us off at the Aylesworth School it took the older pupils on to high school. The next year that included Lydia. She was the first one in our family who had a chance to go to high school. Transportation was impossible to arrange for my older sisters.

My new teacher, Mrs. Titus, was so different from Miss Fisher — much more stern and insensitive to people's needs and feelings. When she said, "Have this ready by tomorrow or I'll cut your head off," I was really scared. I had never heard such talk before. It took me to the end of the year to get used to her threats. The classes went on pretty much as before. Again I had trouble to keep up with the others. I dreaded class, but just assumed that was the way school was and muddled along as best I could. To add to my problem, I came down with scarlet fever. Then Mary got it too and we were quarantined for about a month. That put me back still more and I felt so discouraged. That is when Papa began to help me with my arithmetic. He kept it up until I felt much more comfortable in school. When I was in the third grade on the last day of school I began to have a headache at the all-school picnic. That was when I was coming down with the measles. Mary got measles also. She complained about my bringing bad luck to her with these diseases, but at least this time we didn't have to miss any school.

Mrs. Titus had a son in my room at school. Maybe that is the reason we got some new things. One of them was a sandbox. Most of the time it looked like a table, but on rainy days when we could not go outside to play she took the top off and we could play with sand. It was five or six inches deep and we could make hills and valleys. It was fun.

We now had a music teacher who came to our room once a week to teach us songs and something about the notes in music. (We had a new music teacher almost every year.) When I was in third grade the music teacher started a rhythm band made up of triangles, "sticks," tambourines, and drums. She would put the symbols of these instruments on the blackboard so that we could follow our parts while she played the piano. My instrument was a triangle. The handle I would use to hit the triangle was metal on one side — which made one kind of sound — and wood on the other side for another kind of sound. I remember that Papa burned my initials onto the wooden side.

Mrs. Titus was a divorced woman. She and her son lived with her mother and brother out in the country. One year she invited our whole room to their house for dinner. Her mother cooked the meal and her brother came to get us. This was my first introduction to Jell-O. It was yellow and tasted so good! I think it was Mrs. Titus who initiated and supervised Jell-O sales to raise money toward a "giant stride" for our schoolyard. That was a tall giant pole with a revolving top that had chains hanging down with handles that we children could grasp. We would each take a chain and all run around the pole together to build up some momentum and then hang on to swirl around the pole in a merry-go-round. The school also raised money for this equipment by helping out in some pest-control project I didn't quite understand. I know that the school would get a penny for any mouse tail or sparrow head they would turn in. Each rat tail or crow head would get us ten cents. The name of our principal was Mr. Wallace Aylesworth but the pupils were calling him Wally and he didn't mind. I think that got started because he had two of his brothers in his room. Anyway, Wally and the older boys would take flashlights to a farm home in the evening and ask permission to look for sparrows or other pests in the barn. I was pleased when I could bring a mouse tail to school.

I always liked recess best. Each fall we boys would have fun during out first recesses by going after the gophers. Every summer those lively little brown creatures would make tunnels all over the school yard, making the ground uneven. Wally didn't mind our fight with the gophers, for he wanted a leveled playground. The big boys would take their places at the gopher holes, with bats and clubs in hand. We little fellows were to bring water from the pump by the school entrance. We used the big buckets that had come with some kind of sweeping compound and filled each of them as full as two of us could carry. When some boys poured water into the holes others were ready to club the gophers as they popped out. By the time we got finished with that sport there were no more gophers left—until the next year! We must have gotten rid of twelve or fifteen each fall.

One of the games we played outside when the weather was good was called Zippy. It was played with two pieces of broomstick, one about seven inches long and the other about five or six times that long. We dug a narrow hole in the ground about a foot long and the player would lay the short stick across it. With the long stick he zipped it out over the over the heads of the other players. If the fielder caught the stick the player at the hole was out. If not the fielder would throw the stick back, trying to have it land within a stick's length of the hole. If he succeeded the player was out. Otherwise the player had one more step in his turn and that was to hold the little stick in his hand and bat it out with the long stick. The fun, most of the rules, and the scoring had to do especially with the throw-backs—the guesses, the challenges, the measurements. When the player was put out he would join the fielders and the next player would try his luck at the Zippy hole. Many years later when I lived at Greencroft I revived the game for a session for old times' sake. A newspaper reporter wrote a light-hearted feature about it and took a picture of the old folks arguing about the rules of the game.

We played it less often as time went on. I don't know whether we tired of it or found baseball more fun. Two leading boys would choose up sides by grasping a bat by turns and the one who was able to get to the top and throw the bat the farthest got to choose first. I didn't like to be chosen last, but I couldn't catch or bat very well. We played marbles outside or inside and continued with mumbley-peg and the other usual games.

Two wire fences came together at the corner of our school yard and we youngsters began to thread long grasses thorough the webbing. When we saw how well they held, we began to weave a wall in earnest with long grasses, stalks, and whatever we could find. With two good walls we got the idea of stretching branches or pieces of board over the top and having a real hut. It lasted until one day the farmer decided to burn the dead weeds in his fence row and the fire took our hut as well. Then we went across the road to the woods to build a more ambitious hut made out of branches and stray finds. We made a cozy hut that we were proud of. Meanwhile the older boys had nailed branches to a tree to make a ladder leading up to what was to be a tree house. To our surprise one morning we found that a hobo had actually slept in our little hut! The Aylesworth cornfield was next to the woods and we saw that he had built a fire and cooked roasting ears. We also found an empty baked bean can.

When I was in the fourth grade it was Wally's last year of teaching at our school. He played with the pupils which sometimes included some of us from the other room. As winter came on the pond in the neighbor's field froze over. Wally not only allowed us boys to go there to skate, but even went with us. He and the older boys played ice hockey. A few of the boys had real hockey sticks. The others made sticks out of branches that had usable curves. We younger boys had skates and sleds. Holding our sleds, we would run and then take a belly-flop on the sled and slide along as far as momentum would take us. It was great fun. Wally enjoyed it as much as we did and sometimes the noon hours got pretty long! Once or twice a year on a really cold winter day

Mama would bring a huge kettle of vegetable soup to school. There was a burner in the utility room where she could keep it hot and there was enough tableware there for us to eat it.

Through these years my playmates included congenial boys like Paul Wadsworth, a Methodist boy, and Jackie Aylesworth, and Harold Carlson, who would generously give us rides on his bicycle. Lester Frey was with us when he came to live with his grandparents. I liked to play with him but he always seemed to be rather uncertain and nervous. His parents were divorced. After a year or two he went to live with his mother in Oklahoma. Ronnie Aylesworth and Zelpha Woolever helped us build the huts. The Kisch girls were good playmates too, but they were shy. Their people were recent immigrants and they were used to more urban ways. After a year they moved back to the city.

Sam Ayles had no mother and lived with his father, who could really swear and chewed tobacco. Sam also chewed tobacco and could swear. His lunch bucket was usually full of store-bought cookies which he liked to trade with the rest of us for sandwiches. Another boy came from a troubled family and was a real bully. Once when he was after me and knocked me down, I raised my legs for protection, but lowered them just as he was running over me and they hit him. He ran crying to the teacher, saying I had kicked him in the stomach. I was kept in at recess for punishment but I felt it was worth it. It happened again when he was snowballing me. I had backed up into a snow bank where the snowflakes had partially crystallized and were sharp. My snowball hit his face. Again he went crying to the teacher, saying that I had hurt his eye. Once again I felt enough satisfaction to offset my punishment.

By the time I was in fifth grade and in the other room, Wally's place had been taken by a Mr. Baker. There was a world of difference between the two men. Mr. Baker was probably a better teacher but he was not the kind that would have come out to play with us. I liked it that he let us keep our books open during recitation. Now for the first time we studied American history and I really enjoyed that course.

Mr. Baker had come from southern Indiana and he was especially patriotic. I don't know where our school's flag came from, but he wanted it displayed. There was a tree in Freys' woods that would make a good flagpole, and so he asked Warren Frey, an eighth grader, to bring a team of horses and wagon to school one morning. We boys and Mr. Baker all piled into the wagon and went to get the tree. Mr. Baker chopped it down and the kids peeled off the bark. We energetically hoisted the pole onto the wagon and brought it to the school yard where Mr. Baker dug a deep hole for it. He fastened a pulley to the top and put ropes in place and we all helped set up the pole. Mr. Baker explained how to handle a flag, emphasizing how we never dare let it touch the ground. He trained the oldest boys in putting the flag up and taking it down. Thereafter the boys took turns in doing that every day and Mr. Baker made it an honor to perform this ritual.

Though school was such an important part of my life, I lived and loved the life of a farmboy. My parents assigned me chores just as soon as I was able to do them, beginning with gathering the eggs. Mary and I did that together. If a broody hen stayed on the nest and wanted to peck at us one of us would take a cob and get her attention while the other quickly slipped the eggs out from under her. Early on I had to turn the coffee grinder and also the glass churn. Sometimes I thought the butter would never form, but it always did eventually, and I liked the buttermilk. I still do. Mary and I also had to go get the mail. The mailbox was about a mile away and located at a corner of property owned by the Beekers. There had once been a farmstead at that corner, but now nothing was left but an orchard. The Beekers told us we could pick up whatever apples we wanted, so Mary and I would bring a huge kettle, as large as we two could carry when it was filled with windfall apples.

We had a spring on our farm that fed a low place in our lane and oozed on to the Frey land adjoining ours. The ground was so soft that we put a bridge over the spot, really a kind of platform right on the ground. I don't know why our old horse Tom would not use it one day. He tried to go beside it and immediately began to mire down. The harder he tried to pull himself along, the deeper he sank until he was really stuck. Papa had to tie a rope around him and have the team pull him out.

The water from our spring fed into a kind of trough where it entered the Frey farm. A bit further on it was caught in a tile, but there was always some water available for livestock or any other use. The butcher at Hebron rented that pasture for his cattle and each week he would butcher one of them for meat for his shop. He would come to this spot where water was available and then what would be of no use to him he would leave lying there, hoping that Nature or animals would take care of the "leavings." This was a job for the turkey buzzards. We would see them begin circling high in the air after the butchering day and then after their lunch they would sit on the fence posts. We children were told, "Don't go near those buzzards for they will vomit their food right at you!"

The turkey buzzards weren't the only birds we learned to know in our new location. The farm had so many goldfinches which we called "wild canaries." Now I knew about meadowlarks, bobolinks, and red-winged blackbirds. I could hear the quail calling "Bob White! Bob White!" but I never could see any. The killdeer would lay her eggs on tiny pebbles in the fence row and if we approached the nest she would pretend to be crippled and with drooping wing would try to lead us further away. I liked to see the barn swallows swoop as they caught mosquitoes, or whatever, and I enjoyed seeing their nests plastered against the barn walls.

In our second year in Indiana my sister Della and family also moved into our community, settling on a rental farm a half-mile east of our mailbox. She had married Bill Litwiller (the younger brother of Fannie's husband Eli) and at that time they had one little girl named Doris. The barn had burned down on that property and now a new one was being built. For the first several years he did general farming but he also did blacksmithing on the side. He had learned these skills from his father, a blacksmith in Illinois, and it was so convenient that Bill could shoe horses and satisfy related needs not only for himself but for the community.

Naturally we and they were back and forth a lot. One time he asked me with a wink in his eye whether I would like to drive. Well, of course! I sat on his lap and while he operated the car my job was to steer. I steered him right into the ditch! He walked home to get equipment to get us back on the road, grumbling that he should have known I was too young to drive!

However, it wasn't long until I could ride a horse. When Molly was saddled up and brought along the fence I could get into the saddle by climbing the fence and then crawling over onto her back. When thrashing time came I even had a job to do. The water jug had a strap and handle that could hook over the horn of the saddle and I was the waterboy for the fellows in the field who loaded the wagons. Mr. Beeker saw me do this and asked whether I would be a waterboy for him when his thrashing turn came. I was glad to do it and never thought of any kind of reward. Then he gave me four quarters! I was overjoyed—I was nine years old by then and had earned my first dollar!

But even before I could ride a horse I had a memorable experience with Mr. Beeker. I got to ride with him when he took a wagon of grain to the elevator at thrashing time. We sat high up front on the spring-seat. When we got to the elevator we backed our wagon up to the ground floor. Then a huge fork came out and began to tilt us so that the grain spilled out on the elevator floor. As it slowly tipped more we were raised higher and higher. It was scary but Mr. Beeker held on to me so that I would not fall. What a thrill that was!

We had pleasant relationships with our neighbors. My parents would not allow us to use first names when speaking of the adults. I knew Mr. Ellison as the fellow who liked to have his boys do the farming. The tractors for the most part were big and heavy and used mostly for plowing and preparing the soil. Then came the smaller Farmall that was lighter and could do more things on the farm. Then Mr. Ellison was interested in doing more field work! He was blind in one eye and he had not quite gotten used to this lighter machine. He couldn't manage the corner and drove right down into the ditch. Fortunately he stayed upright and the water was little more than a foot deep. The neighbors chuckled privately as they pulled him out. Sam Ellison was known to be a sympathizer or member of the Ku Klux Klan, then very influential in Indiana. When I asked Mama and Papa what the KKK was, they explained it to me and made it very clear that they didn't agree with the Klan in any way.

Mama had enough daughters to help her with the bigger chores, but when Mrs. Ellison or Mrs. Beeker had to cook dinner for the thrashers Mama was always on hand to help. Mrs. Ellison was German and it was reflected in her speech. She seemed rather shy and ill at ease among people she did not know well, but she was comfortable with Mama. Occasionally, when the Ellisons saw that we had no company on Sunday afternoon, they would invite us to come over.

That was not often, however, for we were seldom alone on Sundays. Our social life centered around the church. After Sunday services we were often invited to another home for dinner, but more often Mama would invite a family or two to eat with us. The Litwillers were with us very often on Sundays and Papa and Bill would play checkers. Lawrence and family might come to visit, especially in spring and fall. They would take Minnie with them to help with their growing family through the summer. She was always glad to go in order to see her Illinois cousins and friends, but also happy to come home in the fall, for she had to work hard those summers.

Now we lived half-way between Papa's relatives in Illinois and Mama's people in Indiana. I was beginning to know more about them, especially through visits. I knew from Mama's addresses on the envelopes that Grandpa Miller was Samuel B. Miller and in later years I learned that my grandmother, his first wife who died young, had been Fannie Miller and that both Miller lines could be traced back to the first Amish settlement in America.

I knew that Mama was from a family of ten children, but that twins, a boy and a girl, had died in infancy. Of the eight daughters that grew up Aunt Lizzie Reinhardt was the oldest, then came my mother, and then Aunt Alice Stalter. I didn't know Aunt Luella very well. She had married Lewis Miller and lived in Michigan. I remember a visit from Aunt Susan Kipfer because Uncle Christ cut out a huge paper circle and continued cutting inside around and around in it until he had a long curved strip. He fastened this to a string and hung it above our domed living room stove. The curly snake kept going round and round under the influence of the warm air coming up. Aunt Katie married Ben Martin and lived in Nebraska. Ben raised horses. He would bring horses to Illinois and make a long visit with the relatives until he got them all sold. Aunt Ida Nafziger had a big family and seldom came to see us. Her husband Jonas never came. She died rather young. Aunt Nellie, the youngest, died just before I was born.

I know now that my most definite immigrant Miller ancestor was Christian Miller who married Franey Mishler. Both were born in Europe and came to America with their parents, in Franey's case her mother Dorothea and her stepfather Christian Zook, who had arrived once before with his first wife and was now on his second trip. (Franey or Vreni was the nickname for Verena, a popular name in Switzerland. In America the name was anglicized in a variety of spellings—Veronica, Feronica, Fronia, Frohnie, Sophronia, Frances, and later the most popular variant, Fannie.) Christian's father is believed to be a Christian Miller, but with the great duplication of names and the lack of adequate documentation, it has not been proved to everyone's satisfaction. Dr. Hugh Gingerich, the best Amish genealogist of our time, thought the evidence is good.[1]

The young couple's first child was born in 1760, and so they must have come to America as teenagers. They apparently settled near Shillington in Berks County, Pennsylvania, for at least one good reference calls him "Shillington Christ" to distinguish him from the other Christian Millers. Their son Abraham, born 1766 and one of eight children, married Anna Hochstetler, a granddaughter in the family that was attacked by the Indians. The story is well-known, having been passed down from generation to generation.

Abraham was the first in a line of Miller men who were lured by "opportunity" as land opened for settlement further west. When his family was very young they moved west to Somerset County, Pennsylvania. He was an Amish minister and became blind in later years. Their son Daniel (b. 1794) married Maria Mast and always stayed in Somerset County. Two of his children moved to nearby Cambria County, but the others all moved west. Son

---

[1] Rachel Kreider added genealogical information to this book drawn from her extensive collaborative research with Hugh Gingerich, published as Gingerich and Kreider, *Amish and Amish Mennonite Genealogies* (Gordonville, PA: Pequea Publishers, 1986).

Joseph (b. 1816) died in Missouri, but he had married Nancy Yoder and they moved to LaGrange County, Indiana, when that Amish settlement was getting started. Their son Daniel P. (b. 1837) was born in Pennsylvania, but grew up in Indiana.

Bessie Miller Hooley, Mama's cousin, wrote a booklet about Daniel P. and outlined his family. Daniel had a roving spirit and the family lived at several places before they left Indiana for Missouri. My grandfather Sam and his older brother Joe were the oldest of the twelve children and had some grim experiences when the family would move and suffer times of severe poverty. They were married by the time the family moved to Missouri for the second time, and they stayed behind. Three of their siblings were mutes. I never knew much about them. The younger ones in the family were nearer the age of my mother in the next generation. She would talk about her uncle Abe, but I don't remember him. Uncle Ed married Lydia Egli of Metamora, Illinois, and we had more connections with that family than any of the others. Their son Roy had come to Kouts before we did. He married and settled there as did his sister. Several of the other siblings lived for two to three years in the Kouts area but then they moved back into their home neighborhoods. Aunt Katie, the youngest of the twelve in that branch, was already a widow by the time I remembered her and her sons would bring her for visits. Thus we would see Mama's extended family from time to time, especially when funerals would bring them near our area.

I never knew much about my Grandma Fannie Miller. She died when my mother was eighteen years old. She was a daughter of Yost Miller and Elizabeth (Hershberger) who had ten children, Yost (1830-1911) was the son of Jeptha (1806-1887), who was married three times and had eighteen children. Jeptha was the oldest of eleven children born to Tobias Miller, who seems to have been the son of Abraham, and there is some evidence that Abraham may have been a brother to "Shillington" Christ, but those relationships have never been proved. With a number of Miller immigrants and such large families, it is not surprising that we can find Millers in practically every Amish settlement in this country today.

However, in 1931 when I was in the fifth grade I had other things on my mind than company and relatives. For a year Papa had tried a different form of farming. Sam Voltmann, who was from Chicago, would often come to our neighborhood farm sales in his truck to buy livestock which he would haul back to the city. I don't know where he got his nickname, but the auctioneer at those sales would cry, "Sold, to Sheeny[2] Sam!" or "Sold! to the Jew!" He and Papa must have been standing together at one of those sales and got to talking about Papa's empty silo. Anyway, it resulted in a deal. Sam would buy herds that would be fattened on our farm. He would pay for the feed and some other expenses and of course would get the profit when the stock was sold. Papa would get $30 a month for managing the process and caring for the cattle.

Now Papa didn't have to worry about whether the corn was dried out enough to suit those at the elevator. The stalks were still greenish when he borrowed a corn binder and went row after row to cut them off and bind them into huge bundles. Then neighbors or hired help would come with hay wagons to pick up the bundles and take them to the silo. There an ensilage cutter had been driven up beside the silo, and when the bundles were thrown into the machine it ground them up and blew the chopped corn through a large aluminum pipe up into the silo. A man inside the silo would spread the ensilage to keep it somewhat even and then when the time came he or someone would add stave by stave to close the opening as needed. Since Papa was a good handyman he could make the extra troughs needed for so many cattle. For a dollar he could get a whole load of scrap lumber at the saw mill.

The herd was sold in February. Sam was losing some property in the city and was rethinking his finances. Papa wasn't making much money under the arrangement and was ready to try something different. Fortunately, at that very time he heard through the Mennonite network and relatives that a rental farm was about to be available, located next to the farm of Lee Sutter. Lee was a second cousin to Papa, but the relationship to our family was closer, since he had married my Uncle John and Aunt

---

[2] In the context of Kouts where there were no Jews it is clear that Clayton did not realize that this was not a nickname, but an offensive ethnic reference.

Lizzie's daughter Iva Reinhardt.

Papa went to investigate. He found a farm of 160 acres in flat land with black, sandy soil, and no muck. He was impressed favorably enough that he took Mama to see it. They thought the buildings were rather run down, and yet no more so than what they were living in right then. The deal was soon made and Papa began, when convenient, to haul farm implements to the new place about sixteen miles away-eight miles east of Kouts and a little south. Relatives were very helpful and on moving day one of them came in a truck to haul the furniture. The move was simple and orderly compared to the other time. Everything went so smoothly that in a day's time, by March 1, we already felt settled — so settled that we could go to school in the next day or two.

The school bus picked up Lydia, Minnie, Mary, and me and then left me off at Lauer School, a one-room country school. Mary was going on to school in Kouts, for Lauer took only the first six grades. The building was of cement blocks with a small bell tower and a pump at the entrance. In the back was a large oak tree and there were two outdoor toilets. The entry was a rather large hall where we could put our wraps and lunch buckets. Inside there was a stove at the back, windows along both sides, and a blackboard across the front. The desks were set in double rows: two pupils sat beside each other but in separate seats. There was no recitation bench, but those seats fastened to the front desks could be pulled down serve as a recitation bench.

I liked the teacher immediately. She made school interesting. She was Mrs. Madalyn Eader and was younger than Mrs. Titus. In those days married women were seldom hired as teachers, but the regular teacher at Lauer, Bertha Drazer, got sick and we were lucky to have such a good and experienced substitute. There were about twenty eight pupils in the whole school and three or four in my grade. I had already caught up with the others at Aylesworth School and now could continue comfortably in the class here too. The children were friendly and came from religious families, ranging from Catholic to Apostolic. There were no bullies. The whole school played together at recess — darebase, anti-over, hide-and-seek. In hide-and-seek if the person who was "it" saw even a little glimpse of you, the two of you would race to base. If you lost, you were "out." I had fun by putting somebody else's cap on the end of a stick and letting a tiny bit show. When the one who was "it" ran to the base where he shouted "One, two, three for Clayton," I could show myself and laugh, shouting "Beefsteak!" Because of his mistake I could run and hide again. I was able to enjoy school right away. The fifth and sixth grades were my happiest times in grade school.

In two months school was out and I could spend more time exploring our new farm. The unique feature was the dredge-ditch that extended all along the south side from our house yard on west for a mile, along our fields and on beyond. On the other side of the ditch lay the road and a clear strip between that and the ditch. On the bank on our side, however, was a lush growth of trees and all kinds of shrubs. Some of them were wild berry bushes and the trees included ash, elm, cottonwood, and others. There were lily pads in the water and various kinds of water weeds grew along the edges. A fence separated our fields from the ditch, but between them was ample room for us and the animals to roam. The cows and horses never attempted to jump across the ditch because the growth was so dense, the bank so steep, and the water at least three feet deep. The drainage ditches were a mile apart and if we wanted to swim we could go to the ditch a mile north, where the water seemed cleaner.

Even so, our ditch water was clean enough that we could see the fish, which were larger and more numerous than in our former ditch. In a shallower spot under the bridge by the road I could see the bluegills work the sand into a place to lay their eggs and I could see them defend their "nest." We did more fishing now and had more fish at meal time. Although I could fish alone, I especially enjoyed fishing with Lee Sutter's boys when they would be watching their cows grazing along the roadside. Sometimes we boys would catch a crayfish. We would pull off the tail, peel off the shell, and use what was left for bait. That fresh white meat would usually lure other fish. Sometimes Papa and I would take the lantern and go fishing after supper. Sometimes Lee and his boys joined us to fish by lantern light. One day Mama even decided to go fishing with whoever was fishing at the time. She caught several bluegills and then hauled in a two-pound carp. She was excited about that and was pleased with herself.

One of my first chores on this farm was to keep the water tank filled for the stock. It was located in the barnyard with a hand pump beside it. I would pump at least three times a day to keep that metal tank full. Since we no longer had a windmill, we had a pump in the kitchen to take care of the household needs, and we also had barrels at various places to catch the rainwater from the eaves, which we used for laundry and similar purposes.

Another job I had was to put feed into the horse troughs in the barn. Twice a day I would count out the corn ears and the right measure of oats to put into each horse's trough. Papa would take care of it in the mornings. I would go with him when he went to feed the pigs in the hog lot. There was a trough about eight feet long along the fence and Papa would pour the kitchen slops into the middle so that the liquid flowed each way and the smaller pigs would have a better chance. In the mixture would also be sufficient condensed buttermilk and as big a portion of wheat middlings as needed.

A job I particularly liked that first spring on the new farm was to help Papa with the planting. He would load bags of seed and fertilizer on the wagon and park it in the field near the ditch. I would open these sacks with Papa's knife and unravel as much of the sewing as necessary. I was proud of having that much control of Papa's knife! When he came to the wagon after a round I would have buckets filled with the grain and fertilizer so that he could save time by dumping the contents into the planter and move on. I could refill the buckets and have them ready quite a while before he finished the round. Therefore I had plenty of time to explore the ditch bank and I developed a deep appreciation of Nature.

I watched the bees buzzing in the tall sweet clover. I heard and saw so many birds that were new to me, including a brown thrasher. I heard the bob-whites and saw one or two. I liked to watch the great blue heron come sailing through the air and then stand on his long legs in a shallow place while he looked for fish. After a little while he would sail away again. I was so sad when Papa told me later that he had found the heron dead on the ditch bank—someone had shot him. Papa had some bitter words to say about a person that found pleasure in killing. I wondered why I saw a certain kind of holes in a rather steep part of the ditch bank. I had so many questions to ask Papa when he would come to the wagon. He could answer them all, telling me what I had seen. He explained that the holes in the bank were for nests for the cliff swallows. He also said that the pencil-thick weed with the hard joints was known as the souring rush. If the stalks were cut and dried in a certain way they made good scrubbing brushes for the pioneers. Later in the summer I could eat the wild raspberries and elderberries, but the wild cherries were too bitter. In the fall I could eat the wild grapes and in the right season we could find mushrooms on the ditch bank.

I watched the fish and frogs. (The frogs I could hear during the night.) I watched a muskrat swimming along with an ear of corn in his mouth. I saw a woodchuck eat his way up a milkweed and once in a while I saw a skunk. The small animals were not only along the ditch. Papa one time came across two foxes in a little hollow in the field. They dashed away but when he came back to the spot they were there again. Again they sprang up and ran away, and we never saw them again. Once Papa saw animal tracks leading to the straw stack. He set a trap and caught a possum. In case the pelt was worth something we took it to a fur dealer. He said it had little value, but he gave me ten cents! Once Papa brought home a six-foot blue racer he had killed. Later we found one in our barnyard. We never had snakes before but now the water snakes were quite common. Mama would go after the garter snakes with the garden rake. Uncle John said there used to be rattlesnakes in the area, but we never saw any. We did once see a coyote.

I did not want summer vacation to end, but I did not dread going back to Lauer School in the fall. I could fit right in and enjoyed it. The bell would call us in. The bell rope came down through a hole in the ceiling to the entrance. If one of the older boys pulled it too hard it sometimes would tip the bell over. Then one of the fellows would climb up to the little tower to set it up again and he would also throw down the balls that had lodged there when we played anti-over.

Mrs. Eader appointed committees to celebrate holidays or recognize special events. I was put on the committee for Halloween. I don't remember much about it. I know that we bobbed for apples and I have a vague memory of some guessing games. I do remember that I was pleased about the experience, for I had never been on a committee before!

One of the games we played outside must have been started by accident and it did not last long. Somehow a huge box or a kind of platform had been left on the school ground. A boy would jump up on it and declare, "I'm King of the Hill!" Then the rest of us would try to push him off. He would try to fight us off, but he would never know where the greatest force would be coming from. The one most successful in pushing him off was the winner and would take his turn and declare himself King. The tussle would begin again. I can't recall whether anybody really got hurt, but when I was pushed off as King, I hit my head and had a very bad headache the rest of the afternoon.

Our school building was located at a corner where two roads intersected. On each side of the school yard were dry ditches, the ones along the roads being less deep than the other two. One day the sheep in the pasture across the road broke through the fence and came into the school yard. The son of the owner began to tease the ram and it took after him. He ran for a road ditch and lay flat on the narrow bottom. The befuddled ram could do nothing but jump over him. We had a good time rounding up the sheep and getting them back into the field again.

I remember that we boys found a kind of break in the deeper ditch bank and got the idea of enlarging it into a cave. We dug energetically, thinking what fun it would be to be in a cave. Then one of the fathers found out about it. He reminded us of the dangers of a cave-in and we had to stop. There was a woods nearby and we boys began to explore in it. We found a little sassafras tree and remembered that sassafras was used for tea. While chewing on the flavorful twigs we enthusiastically began to dig until we had a piece of root for each of us to take home for tea. By that time Mrs. Eader found out about it and that fun was also stopped suddenly. She said she was responsible for us and we had to stay on the school grounds.

I was getting along well in the sixth grade until February I came down with pneumonia. I was very sick—so sick that I missed a whole month of school before I was well enough to return. To add to my misfortune, I developed a severe pain toward the end of the term. First I had a headache that kept getting worse and worse through the day and a pain started in my abdomen that kept getting sharper and sharper. My sisters said that I moaned all night. When I was no better in the morning my parents called the doctor. He diagnosed it immediately as appendicitis and said I needed an operation as soon as possible. For some reason he didn't like the nearest hospital which was in Valparaiso, but arranged for me to go to LaPorte, about thirty miles away. Lee Sutter drove the car taking me and my parents to the Holy Family Hospital. I was so miserably sick and scared.

When the doctors examined me they found that my appendix had burst. The operation was successful, but as I came to I was sick from the ether. I felt like I had to vomit but there was nothing to come up. I had what some people call the "dry heaves." Mama stayed with me that night, but she soon had to go home. My parents couldn't come see me very often but I was recovering well and receiving such good care that I felt safe and secure. I could relax and take in what was happening in these strange surroundings.

This was my first experience with Catholics. The nurses were nuns and they wore black dresses with white at the top front. They were so kind to me and gave me a book to read with the title *Navarre of the North*. It was the story of a hunter and a life that was very new to me. The nurses would crank up the head of my bed so that I could sit up to eat. The food was good, but I was not hungry. I was so astonished when they served good fruit on a lettuce leaf with dressing and called it salad. The Catholic priest came by regularly and asked how I was doing. He wore a black shirt and a white collar that went all the way around the front. A boy named Norman, who was a little older than I, for some reason came to the hospital often after school and he would talk to me. All this helped pass the time pleasantly. My doctor was a quiet, sober man, but he rubbed behind my ear and found a half dollar! He did that twice more and each time found a coin. I got to keep the half dollar, the quarter, and the dime.

My recovery went well and at the end of two weeks my parents came to take me home. I lay across the back seat, all huddled up in blankets. At first I had to be careful about lifting and any other movement that would strain my incision, but I began to gain weight and feel more normal. By the time I was ready to return to school the pupils were already ten days or more into summer vacation. I was pleased that they had not forgotten me. One day the teacher had come with a basket of fruit with several Hershey bars mixed in—what a treat!

The summer soon passed and it was time for school again. This time I was going into the seventh grade at the Kouts School. Now came another time of frustration and strain. I had missed so much school and was again behind the others in class. This was a town school and there were so many more pupils. The classes seemed so large—one class larger than the whole Lauer School—and the atmosphere seemed so impersonal. The seventh and eighth grades shared a room, the seventh graders on the right side of the room and the others on the left. When one had a class in the home room, the other teacher had a class elsewhere. I didn't know when or where to go, but I watched the other Lauer pupils and followed them.

To add to my uneasiness, I now felt conspicuous—my four front teeth were missing. I had become used to it, but now I realized how I must look to strangers. When the doctor examined me in connection with my appendectomy, he exclaimed, "Why, he still has his baby teeth!" He recommended that those front teeth come out so that the permanent teeth could grow in more easily and normally. The dentist agreed and removing them was not much of an ordeal. I noticed the inconvenience most during the roasting ear season and I didn't think much about it until now when the town kids—not my Lauer friends—began to tease me and call me Grandpa. That hurt. I didn't tell anyone how embarrassed and discouraged I felt, but stumbled along as best I could.

At recess we no longer played the games we used to play. We mostly just stood around and talked, glad for the break in routine. Despite a stress on exercise there was no gymnasium or physical education. Even pupils going home for lunch were encouraged to get back promptly and take part in soccer or volley ball. I remember that we boys sometimes played around with a huge medicine ball. But first we boys who carried our lunches would eat in the boiler room where Mr. Frey, the janitor, had his desk and chair. He was a friendly man and a good story teller. He had been a hunter in his day and I liked to hear him tell of his experiences. He knew the swamps very well before they were drained and he could coach and guide other hunters, some of whom came from as far away as Chicago.

We were very fortunate in seventh and eighth grades to have two good teachers. Miss Loretta Lauer seemed to have the most seventh grade classes. The Lauers were a very prominent family in the community. The Lauer School was named for them and they had an important grocery-drug store on Main Street. Her specialty was history and civics. When we studied Indiana history I especially enjoyed the stories she could tell about the people and events that had to do with our local area. Like Mr. Frey, she could tell stories about Linc Arnold, the hermit who lived in the swamps and would pull his own teeth. Miss Lauer was a very patriotic person and would tell us stories about the war (World War I), which was the war to save democracy. She was very proud of her brother who had served in the war and brought back home various souvenirs like hand grenades and different sizes of shells. It brought home to me the horror of war. Sometimes at night I could hardly sleep, troubled by worrisome and upsetting thoughts about a dangerous and warlike world.

Mr. Thomas Eader, husband of my Lauer School teacher, taught math, English, and any eighth grade subjects like general science, which I liked. In his literature class he would read books to us and I especially remember Jack London's *The Call of the Wild*. Mr. Eader was also coach for high school athletics. When he saw any promising talent in his classes he would encourage them to train for the ball teams. No doubt that is why Kouts took three out of four county championships.

Once a week a music teacher would come to our room and if there were special speakers or occasions we would all meet in the auditorium for what we called Assembly. I can't remember much about all that but I do remember that I wasn't the only one who couldn't pipe up and respond in class as well as expected, for one day Mr. Eader exclaimed, "I might as well be talking to twenty-four fence posts!" As I moved into the eighth grade I found school much easier. I had made some adjustments and felt better caught up with the others. My teeth were late in coming in but in general I found school to be more pleasant. Even so, I still think it would have been better for me if I had repeated the sixth grade.

In the third year that we lived on that farm my enjoyment of the ditch was completely destroyed. All the lush growth on the ditch bank was removed, leaving uneven mounds of dirt and covered debris. The scene looked bleak and bare. The reason given for all this did make some sense. The ditch was to be dredged again to make the channel deeper and free of unwanted accumulations of stuff so that the drainage water could flow more easily to the Kankakee River five miles away.

As much as I hated to see so much of Nature destroyed I had to admit that I found the whole procedure to be very interesting. First the trees were cut down. They crashed over the fence into our fields. The fence was so old and unnecessary that we never replaced it. The logs were our property and so Papa put chains around them, the large branches and any of the wood that might have future use, and the horses pulled them into our wood lot. Anything left that would not burn and had no use whatsoever was left on the bank and was covered with dredging. That included the stumps, which had been dynamited and blown up in great blasts of sand. As the dredge machine crawled slowly along it dug up the most interesting things. I could see how long and intertwined the root system had been for the water lilies. At one place it brought up what was left of an old boat. When the old wooden bridge near our house had been replaced years earlier, the pilings had been left to rot in the water. We were given that wood too, which was so sulfur-soaked that after it was dried and put into our stoves it burned with a blue flame. With the better connection to the river the fish soon returned and we could go on with our fishing. There were so many turtles. One man told us boys he would give us ten cents for any turtle we caught, but he never returned and we didn't catch any either.

Later on, when really cold winter set in, the ditch would freeze over in some spots, but not everywhere. There were some places where the ice was very thin or there was none at all. It happened that one time a large flock of mallard ducks found such a place and Papa was able to shoot several before they got away. Before long they were back and he could get a few more. By the end of the day he could bring in seventeen ducks! With so many he called his son-in-law Bill Litwiller, who was glad for a share. For a time we had several wonderful stuffed duck dinners, a holiday kind of treat. Eventually some of the water weeds came back and we saw sweet clover again. We put out some melons on the ditch bank but the muskrats and other little animals enjoyed them too much for us to try gardening there again.

These years were very hard for us on the farm. The farmers felt the Depression several years before it hit the nation as a whole. To begin with, we had several very hot, dry summers and the crops did not do well. One year the chinch bugs, little black and white bugs not much bigger than a fly, got into our corn fields and ate into the stalks which were nourishing the bugs more than the corn ears.

Then one year when the crops were flourishing and looked promising, a terrific hail storm suddenly burst on us and did untold damage. The corn was already in tassel, but the hail riddled the tassels so that pollination was poor and the yield had too many little nubbins. The oats went down so flat that they could not be saved. We disked the field and sowed buckwheat because it could mature in a much shorter growing season. I remember how busy the bees were in that field and how the blossoms had a sweet yet strong odor. When we threshed the buckwheat we had some of the grain ground into flour. We enjoyed the buckwheat pancakes very much! The farm animals obviously liked the buckwheat straw too. Ruth Baughman Unrau, who was in Lauer School with me, later moved to Kansas and became a recognized Mennonite author. One of her first books, *Buckwheat Summer*, told the story of that year.

Mr. Heininger, our landlord, lost the farm and the mortgage was held by the Prudential Mutual Life Insurance Company. Eventually they decided to get it ready to sell and began to fix up the buildings. First they repaired the corncrib and chicken house. Finally they put a new roof on the crib and the barn and reshingled the house.

Our Mr. Heininger was not as much of an entrepreneur as his bachelor brother who had lived on our farm before we moved there. Now he was living about fifteen miles away and had an idea that he thought would help not only himself but the community. He rented land to raise turnips and beans on a large scale. He put out at least thirty acres of green beans. When they were ready for table use he sent out a call for pickers at a dollar a day. People quickly responded and they came by the busload from as far away as Gary and Hammond. They were glad to get a little cash and we youngsters were especially glad, for we had no other chance to earn anything. One girl came who had just one arm, but she could keep up with the rest of us. I would drag my half-bushel basket along the row and when I got to the end of it I dumped my beans into the truck. No matter how tired I would get I willingly worked for my dollar a day and was so glad I had accumulated enough to buy my clothes for high school as well as most of my books. This Mr. Heininger also planted soup beans. Whatever green beans did not get picked he let ripen and then mixed them with the soup beans. They were harvested with a binder and the bundles threshed while the pods were still firm enough that the beans did not shell out beforehand. He paid the thresher help in beans. That was a year when we had a generous supply for all winter!

As the Depression dragged on, the strain and stress became deeper all across the country. We of course had the farmers' point of view. By then Franklin D. Roosevelt had been elected President. We were well aware of that since we were Democrats surrounded by Republicans. It seemed that no matter what disappointment or misfortune occurred the President's political foes put the blame on him.

During preceding years when farm prices began to go down, many famers plowed up more land in order to produce more and keep the profits up. Now the overproduction was also affected by trade and tariff regulations, so that the supply was greater than demand. The method promoted by Henry Wallace, the new Secretary of Agriculture, provoked great disagreement. He urged letting land lie fallow and reducing the sale of hogs, for example. Kill pigs! Waste land! Many farmers saw no sense to that. Papa, however, was willing to cooperate. We raised no hogs to sell and he left some fields uncultivated. Representatives from the government committee came out to measure the land and explain the regulations and the subsidy farmers were to get to compensate for their losses. The subsidy part looked so good to some farmers that they let their most unproductive fields lie fallow. The new TVA (Tennessee Valley Authority) was producing electricity and sending lines across the country. The REA (Rural Electrification

Administration) reached into our community, but only the farmers who owned land could hook into it.

During wheat harvest one year we had to hire help but could hardly afford it. A young man was willing to work for thirty dollars a month—a dollar a day—for it gave him a job and he wanted to be in our neighborhood for personal reasons. On rainy days he couldn't work and earn his dollar but he lived with us and could have his board and room. Carrie and Bessie, working for wealthier people in Valparaiso, were getting better wages—ten dollars a week—and they generously helped us when it was so hard for us to meet expenses.

That helped us in other ways as well. For instance, when the wealthy hostesses they were working for would have them trim off the crusts when making sandwiches, it was expected that those crusts would be discarded. However, my sisters would bring them home and Mama would add enough onions and other ingredients to make good bread stuffings for us. It was also assumed that the cooks would throw away such things as meat fryings, but my sisters carefully saved these too, as Mama could use them to make good soups and gravies. Mennonite maids were in demand and therefore when my sisters applied for jobs and asked not to work on Sundays they readily got permission. Papa often went to Valparaiso on Saturday evenings to bring the girls home for Sunday. Thus they could bring us those discards while they were still fresh. For a year's supply of flour we took our wheat to the elevator at Francesville, about fifteen miles away. They would explain to us how much flour they would give us for each bushel of wheat.

When our church sent out calls for produce for the mission in Chicago the response was good. Our family too loaded the back of our car with as much as we could share. In our town the WPA (Works Progress Administration) hired men who needed jobs to help build a new school. The idea was well received and earned general satisfaction, but in other places there was loud complaint that the government was hiring men too lazy to work—that men leaning on their shovels were making WPA a huge boondoggle. No doubt the project employed a lower level of the work force, putting men to work that may never have held a job before. In all this mix of misunderstanding and disagreement, promise and some progress, it made for an atmosphere of uneasiness as well as hope.

Through all the strain of "hard times" and uncertainty my parents were good role models. They did not complain or indulge in undue discussion about misfortune or disappointments. They did their best to analyze situations and to see differing points of view. They always had hope for the future. It was during this time when our names for them changed. When Lydia went to high school she told us that people considered the names of Papa and Mama too childish for adults to use. We therefore began to say Pop and Mom, as our friends were doing. Our older siblings thought that did not show enough respect for our elders. We settled for Pop and Mom when we were talking to outsiders but around home we continued our usual Papa and Mama, especially when addressing them.

During these years I went to church regularly, listening to the sermons, singing along with the congregation, and enjoying the Sunday fellowship the rest of the day. Now at church I was sitting with the boys near my age. On Sunday evenings at Young People's Meeting I would recite my Bible verse. It always included the "text word," the word chosen by the denominational leadership to go with the theme of the evening.

It was a time when the churches particularly stressed foreign missions and there were special efforts to get children interested and involved. We were given quarters to "invest" and then we would bring our coins and the "profit" back to the Mission Fund. One year Mary and I bought two dozen duck eggs with our quarters. We divided them into three nests which we had cleaned and provided with fresh straw. It was not hard to find three broody hens, for we always had some that wanted to stay on the nests to hatch out little chicks. They didn't seem to know or care that they were sitting on duck eggs. When the eggs were hatched the hens still took care of the strange little chicks that wanted to get into the water every chance they had! Between the nests and us, we got the ducklings to grow until time to sell them. But first we plucked the fine white feathers on their breast: they made such a good pillow! We happily doubled our money and brought in our profits.

One year I bought a pig from a neighbor with my four quarters. I doubt whether he was a very good farmer, for I heard Papa say that the pig would have died if I hadn't taken it. It had a skin disease which we treated with sheep dip. It must have burned him, for he circled around and around. He finally quieted down and the skin cleared. He actually became a good pet and I called him Sammy. When I would start to scratch his belly he would promptly lie down, asking for more of it. I brought him up to 200 pounds. At two and a half cents a pounds I was able to turn my one dollar into five, which I proudly brought to the Mission Fund.

At about the age of twelve the children began to think seriously about joining the church. At least once a year some evangelist would come in to hold a series of meetings. At the end of the later services, during an invitational hymn, those ready to make a commitment would stand. J. E. Hartzler was a dynamic speaker and when he came to the General Conference church our family went to hear him. He preached on the wages of sins and so dramatically went through the suffering of an unrepentant sinner as he was experiencing punishment that I became very upset and actually scared. I wanted so much to be among the saved and join God's people, but I wanted to be in my own church and did not stand.

I was uneasy in the following weeks and months. I so recently had twice been near death and especially during such a time as a severe thunder storm I would be reminded of my mortality and my condition "outside the fold." In time an evangelist came to our church and as soon as the invitation was given I stood up. In our congregation it happened that there were youngsters just older than I and some just younger so that I was the only one that season to join the church and there was no "instruction class." The minister simply met with me during several Sunday school hours to explain Mennonite beliefs.

Several Sundays later I was baptized, with the usual ritual used in Mennonite churches. I sat in the front row during the regular service. At the end of it the bishop, who had preached the sermon, came down to where I was sitting. He was Mama's uncle Dan Miller but was known throughout the conference as D.D. I rose and he asked me five or so questions—about turning away from worldly things, my belief in Jesus Christ, whether I was willing to "give and receive counsel," and so on. I could answer yes to each one. By this time the deacon was beside us with a pitcher of water. The bishop cupped his hands and the deacon poured some water into them. He then opened them on my head and the water ran from his fingers. He did this three times —"in the name of the Father," and "the Son," and the third time "the Holy Ghost." He then extended his hand as I rose. This was the "right hand of fellowship" extended to a member of the congregation, and then he gave me the "holy kiss." (See Romans 16:16).

This was also a turning point in my Sunday School experience. Younger children's classes were held in the basement, where Aunt Lizzie was superintendent. Since Mennonite women at that time could not hold official positions in the church, Amos Birky had the title of Superintendent of Children's Sunday School, but he himself said, "Lizzie does all the work." Now as a member of the church I moved up to the balcony, where others in the middle-school age had their class. In another year or two we would be moving down into the sanctuary where people seated themselves according to their classes as soon as they arrived. Each class required a bench or two and they would be located next to one another. At class time the teacher would crowd in to stand facing the front bench. The teachers tried to keep their voices down so that only their own class could hear, and yet with all of them speaking at once there was a general low chatter all over the big room until the superintendent up front tapped the bell on the pulpit to announce the end of class time.

Mama taught Sunday school as far back as I can remember. At first she had classes of younger women but in my time she was teaching the old ladies in the front left-hand amen corner, a position she had until her stroke. Mama was always a good church worker. I remember that she was the first to bring flowers to the church. She had always been good with flowers and she had beautiful flower beds. One Sunday when she thought of how plain and bare the church looked, she arranged a large bouquet and put it on a little stand in front of the pulpit. When no one objected, she continued to do that whenever she could.

She also found her unique place of leadership. In our area there were three churches of our branch of Mennonites—Kokomo, Kouts, and Burr Oak, a smaller church near Rensselaer. These churches kept in touch with each other, especially twice a year. Every year there would be a Thanksgiving service at Kokomo and we were all invited. The young people especially liked to attend, not only to "get away" but there were many more young people at Kokomo and Kokomo-Kouts marriages occurred. Those who could not conveniently go could attend the local services, which were shorter and more informal.

However, the Sunday School Conference was a much larger affair. It was held every May 30, every other year at Kokomo and in the alternate year either at Kouts or Burr Oak. It drew speakers from all three churches and we would be sure to go to Kokomo if one of my sisters was on the program. When it came to our church Mama was always especially involved. Since she did not drive a car, she did not attend the monthly Sewing Circle meetings. Nor did she do very much in connection with Fourth of July picnics, but at Conference time she was at the forefront of hostessing and arranging for the big dinner. She was a very good cook and one year when the women decided for all to make one kind of fruit salad it was Mama's recipe they used.

I always looked forward to those dinners and to the fellows that I would meet. We had to attend the programs that were in progress, but as soon as we could be released we enjoyed the dinner and just jollying around with each other. Usually we also had spirited discussion as to who would win the Indy 500 races held on that day in Indianapolis. We knew very little about it but we could express opinions just the same.

One of the high points of the year in my boyhood that I especially looked forward to was butchering day. It usually came toward the end of January or early February when the weather would be cold and there was less chance of contaminating the meat. On that day I would stay home from school. This was a family affair that reached beyond our household with as many as six or seven families represented. Papa had the equipment, the skills, and the most knowledge about butchering pigs in general, so he was always the leader, no matter at whose house the butchering took place.

He would start the fire under the scalding trough early in the morning so that the water would be boiling by the time we needed it. When it was time to shoot the pig, he knew the exact spot in the forehead where the shot was to go. He would then bleed it, starting while it was still lashing around, and then the dead pig would be dragged through the scalding trough. After that it would be pulled out onto a table where helpers on both sides would begin the big job of scraping off the bristles and outer skin, down to the filmy inner skin. Then Papa would hook the legs on to a tripod so that the head hung down. He would cut off the head and a helper would take out the brains and get the head started on a collection of meat that would be cooked before grinding. The huge kettle was already in place in the outdoor fireplace and one of my first jobs was to keep the fires going in both places.

Papa would make the important slit down the side of the pig and he would take out the heart, the liver, and intestines. By then I was on hand as the errand boy with the dishpan to collect and take them to the places where they should go. The large intestine was discarded, but the small intestines I took to the kitchen, where Mama and her helpers would turn them inside out and scrape and clean and scrape and clean, over and over, until they were ready for the sausage stuffer later in the day. It was no wonder that Papa's sausage was so good, for he saved the tenderloin for it as well as the trimmings from the special cuts. All these things were collected in a tub to be ground without any cooking. Most of the other parts, like heart, liver, head meat, tongue, and so on went into the big iron kettle. Cooking also made it easier to take meat off the bones.

During all this activity, Papa knew just when to shoot the next pig so that the process would go on without delay or undue interruption. Papa would also cut out huge slabs of fat which was to be cut up into walnut-sized chunks for rendering lard later.

This was a good early job for me or perhaps for some novice who felt more comfortable doing that rather than any other part of the process which he knew nothing about.

When the meat in the big kettle was thoroughly cooked it was taken out, deboned and ground and then taken back to the kettle again for reheating. By that time the broth had been boiled down so much that the mixture had to be stirred to keep it from scorching. The finger test decided when it was hot, but not too hot, to pour into crocks as liverwurst. When it would cool down enough grease would have come to the top to congeal and seal the contents until we used them.

At noon all activity stopped while we gathered around the table for a big dinner which included fresh-fried brains, sweetbreads, and liver. One of the last tasks was to stuff the casings with the choice meat collected in the tub which by now had been ground and seasoned. Lee Sutter owned the sausage stuffer and therefore had the critical job of getting the meat flowing smoothly while someone was turning the crank. People began going home in the afternoon, taking with them a good supply of fresh sausage for supper. Characteristic of Mama, she would also see to it that a generous supply would be in the mailbox the next day for the carrier.

If there had been no time to render the lard earlier our own family would attend to that after the others had left. The kettle was thoroughly cleaned and put back over the fire again to melt the little chunks of fat. When they were melted and hot we would toss in the filmy inner skin of the pig which promptly fried into what we called cracklings. We liked to nibble on these, but they were usually fed to the chickens or used otherwise on the farm. Not a thing went to waste. Even the ears were skinned and put into the liverwurst, but we put the feet and tail into the brine barrel. The brine barrel was a job that could wait for the next day. The barrel, which may have been a rain barrel, was thoroughly cleaned and the hams, shoulders, and then the side-meat (bacon) were put into it. A huge bucket was filled with water and enough salt added to float an egg. It usually took two such bucketsful to bring the water in the barrel to the right level. Then at the top we put in the pigs feet, sawed pieces of backbone and such odds and ends which would be eaten first. I usually got the tail.

I kept the job as errand boy through the years but as I became older and stronger I got more responsibilities beyond fetch-and-carry and keeping up the fires. Papa as the coordinator would assign me to stir or scrape or fit in wherever convenient. Raising and processing meat for the season was an important farming operation and we always enjoyed a special day of good family togetherness along with it.

Mama was in charge of what happened to the meat after butchering day. As warmer days approached and we had eaten the meat at the top of the brine barrel, she took the other pieces to be smoked. She used our cob house (where we stored corn cobs to use as kindling for fires) for a smokehouse and hung the pieces from hooks. She built a fire in a worn-out tub and then covered the hot coals with apple wood or hickory chips to keep the fire alive, but have it smoke and smolder. The meat had already been cured, but this added to the flavor. After a week or so she would wrap each piece in paper and put it in one of the paper flour sacks which she had been collecting through the winter. She tied each tightly and hung in the coolest place we had until we could use it.

It was sometime during these years before I went to high school that Grandpa Miller came to live with us. My last reference to him in this story was when his father's family was moving to Missouri for the second time, but he was not going along. He was married by then and had one or two children. He stayed in Indiana most of his married life, although Aunt Luella was born in Michigan.[3] We can assume that Grandpa was as interested in trying out what looked like financial opportunities as some of his relatives had been. They were back in Indiana in 1894 when Aunt Nellie, the youngest, was born, but they must have moved to Illinois soon after that. Grandma Miller died there in 1898. I'm sure his older daughters were keeping house for him until he married a widow in 1900. She was a Mrs. Jacob Eash whose maiden name had been Mary Hochstetler. She was from Indiana and so Grandpas moved back there along with his daughters that were still at home. The stepmother, who had not had any

---

[3] in 1884 at Mancelona, Antrim County, east of Traverse City.

children of her own, did not seem to be in any mood to raise a family of daughters. The older girls felt pushed out and went back to Illinois, using their older siblings as a base while working in other households.

My first memory of Grandpa and Grandma Miller was when Lawrence took Mama and me to see them when I was five years old. They lived across from the Middlebury Creamery. Grandpa took a can of milk across the road to the creamery every morning and I got to ride along with the can on the wheelbarrow.

Grandpa's second wife died in 1930. Lydia went to keep house for him that summer. He either sold or lost his farm and then began a restless transition time for him that was inconvenient for all involved. He began living with one child or another, always with big ideas of how he might make money. When he lived with a granddaughter there was a time when he wanted to make ponds to raise bullfrogs. Then again he decided to paint barns for a living. The farmers were in no position to think of painting barns. When plans had to be made for more permanence for Grandpa it seemed natural that he would come to live with us.

He happened to come when he could be of help to us, for Papa was sick with a serious case of blood poisoning. He was making a little hog house for a sow and her litter. He was bracing a panel against his knee, not expecting the nail he was driving would come through and pierce his skin. After a few days the infection showed up and began to spread up his leg. The doctor would lance one spot after another as time went on and the poison persisted. He later said he thought he had been challenged to save a leg but realized it was to save a life!

When Grandpa came he could help with the chores as well as other little ways that came up. One job he had could last indefinitely and that was to cut wood. This was connected with my assignment to keep the wood boxes filled. That was a real task in the winter. One of the relatives had timber on his land and Uncle John Reinhardt had a buzz saw. We all could have an adequate supply of wood and so Grandpa always had something to do. And we could see that it had to be done his way!

He had a room at our house, ate at our table, went to church with us, and in every way was a member of the family. He did us a good turn when he let the men at church know in what condition Papa really was. In the spirit of real Mennonite mutual aid, they came out and harvested our corn for us that year. We really appreciated what he had done, but as time went on he did not endear himself to us. He had strong opinions and did not hesitate to express them. How often he kept talking when Papa wanted to read the newspaper! Papa said it was a good thing the Lord gave Grandpa only girls to raise, for he was pretty hard on boys. They were to get out into the world early, work hard at something practical, and earn money. He had no patience with a boy going to high school. He would not scold me directly, but he saw to it that I could hear him speak his mind.

Grandpa hated dogs—all dogs. It happened that a short-haired little dog had found its way to our farm and just stayed. She was a cute little thing and I called her Rosie. She and I became good friends. One day when I was standing near the woodpile I saw Rosie asleep. Then Grandpa came along with his ax. Something about a dog sleeping at his woodpile gave him what I considered an evil look, and he hit her with his ax. He killed her! I was shocked speechless. He never apologized or explained his impulse, although I think he did murmur something about her being "just a slut." There wasn't anything to say about it. The dog was dead.

Grandpa was a great talker and he especially had things to say about the "end times" and the writing of the books of Daniel and Revelations. He seemed to think he could have preached like his brother D.D. Sometimes after the sermon at church he would rise in the amen corner and offer his thoughts, especially about prophecy. In the olden days, when there would be several preachers on the bench, one of them would rise after the sermon and testify to the truth the good brother had just offered. Maybe even the second one would do so. Whether Grandpa remembered any such custom or not, he would rise and talk on and on, not aware or not caring how restless the congregation was getting. As he went on and on Mama and Aunt Lizzie would be so embarrassed, and so were his grandchildren! We children could talk to each other about Grandpa getting childish, as we felt old folks often did, but we were to respect our elders and called it "hardening of the arteries" to others.

Mama used to let the broody hens sit on their nests until they hatched out the chicks from the eggs they had accumulated. We therefore had tiny flocks of little chickens running around at various times. Once my parents decided to raise chicks more systematically and sent for 200 chicks which they raised by brooder house. As they grew up the cockerels made for good eating and the pullets began laying eggs. One morning when Papa went out to feed them he found only a scrawny little rooster left and a few hens. Whoever stole those chickens knew we no longer had a dog to warn us. We had our suspicion. It is true that in those hard times stealing chickens was more common than usual, but we had reasons for our special suspicion.

That year we also raised potatoes to sell. They were bringing in a dollar a bushel. We dug a wagon load of them and buried them in a pit on the ditch bank to wait for a time more favorable to sell them. Once again, when we went to get them out we found them gone! And again we thought we knew who had stolen them, but we said nothing about it. We felt we did not have hard enough evidence and under the circumstances an accusation would not gain anything. Not long afterward the suspect moved away, and there were no more thefts after that!

Moving into high school was not as great an adjustment for me as it had been to enter town school. I was now familiar with my surroundings and knew better what to expect. In this particular year it seemed there was an air of excitement in the whole high school because there had been such a change in teachers. Even the principal was new. The general atmosphere was changing and even we pupils had a sense that the level of teaching was being upgraded, and I was especially engrossed in my new courses.

My favorite became biology. The only teacher that had been retained was the one who taught domestic science and biology. We cut up a fish, a crawdad, a frog, a grasshopper. It all was so fascinating. I had chosen Latin and that too opened a new kind of information for me. Our teacher, Mr. Meltzer, was a big, heavy-set man with a hearty laugh. He was not particular about pronunciation, for he said we would never speak Latin. Instead he showed us the Latin origin of many root syllables in our own language and the meanings of prefixes and suffixes. Sometimes there was a whole story or myth behind a single English word or name. Nor was he so concerned about the fine points of grammar, so that when he got sick later in the term and his wife took over we were in for a shock. She was so particular about word endings and grammar in general and precise about pronunciation. My grades plummeted from an A to a C. It was such a relief when Mr. Meltzer could return toward the end of the year. Algebra was another course that was very new to me. I had always liked math, but we were going at it so differently from the way we did arithmetic. I remember that we also had courses like commercial law and salesmanship.

I took part in hardly any extracurricular activities but I did participate in one evening program. Our new music teacher varied what was done in her classes, so that she was training different combinations of singing and instrumental groups, even an orchestra, during school time. I became part of the Boys' Glee Club and we learned so many songs in class that we could give a full evening program for our parents.

I did not participate in any sports, but I was lucky in getting to see many of the baseball games. Usually the buses would take us country kids home right after school, but some of us had a fortunate advantage. Several drivers had brothers on the team and when games were scheduled right after school they managed to linger long enough that we could see much of the game and still get home soon enough to do our chores.

I remember the excitement we had one evening on one of those school bus rides. We were going along as usual and had just stopped to let off a pupil. When we started up again suddenly one corner of the bus went down and we saw a bus wheel roll merrily down the road ahead of us. No one was hurt, but the sudden jolt and drop really got us excited. The slant of the bus was not so severe but the driver made us all stay on the bus until another bus could finish its route and then come for us. By that time we had cooled down and were very ready to get home.

Another event that I remember relating to the bus was in connection with a severe winter storm. The principal got word of the approaching storm and asked all bus pupils who had any connection with people in town not to try to go home by bus. I had no one in town that I could stay with, but Lydia did not live far out in the country and I decided I would walk out to their house. By the time I got to the edge of town the storm was already so strong and the air so cold that I knew I could not make it. I phoned from the filling station and my brother-in-law, Orie, soon came for me. Papa found out through the Lee Sutter boys next day where I was and he phoned. He said I was needed at home to help with the wood and he was coming to get me. It was twenty below zero and of course the car would not start. My parents did what they had done before in such a situation—they hitched the horses to the car and while Mama drove the team Papa kept working the choke and gas lever until the car limbered up and started! We learned later that the school bus could not get that far on the route. The driver took the remaining pupils to his parents' home where his mother took care of them until the roads were opened three days later.

We especially liked our English teacher, Miss Dittmer, and we were so glad that she was our class sponsor. Toward the end of our sophomore year she gave us a party one evening. She lived with her parents and her mother helped hostess our group. I can't remember many details about that party, but I know that I enjoyed the food and games, especially a game called Cootie that was played with dice. I had never heard of it before. I got to this evening party by riding with a neighbor boy who was already old enough to drive.

I also was able to attend the Literary, for Forrest Sutter by now had his driver's license and would take me along. Because I was a freshman at school I was eligible to attend these Mennonite social gatherings held twice a month. I had heard about the Literary as soon as we moved to Indiana, since my sisters were immediately involved and it had sometimes met at our home. When the automobiles came in and young people had much more mobility in getting around, Mennonite leaders were alert to the fact that the young folks would be tempted to go to places they didn't approve of, especially the movies. The suggestion took hold that churches should provide Literary Societies — good, safe occasions where young Mennonites could get together for fun and fellowship related to some educational efforts, giving experience in speaking before an audience, and offering good opportunities for dating. Our Literary also included the young people from the General Conference Church (the Egli Mennonites).

Committees would plan the program and recreation. As a new member I was not asked to take a serious active part. I could contentedly watch others perform and then I would happily enter into the games — Upset the Fruit Basket, Pass the Scissors, Black Magic, and many others. Then I would thoroughly enjoy the refreshments which would be supplied by the host family. On Sunday mornings word would be passed around as to where the next Literary would be and I would look forward to it.

The Literary and our Sundays at home made up my social life, my real relationships beyond my family. We usually had company on Sundays. The Litwillers or other relatives might be with us. My sisters' boyfriends might be there. Mama might invite some family from church. After one of her good dinners we would play various board games. Dominoes were especially popular. Later we would always have popcorn and the girls might make candy. This social life suited me very well. I didn't demand much or expect too much, which helped me feel satisfied and contented. As I look back, I realize that I had a happy childhood. I was safe, secure, and loved. Now my voice was changing. My teeth were coming in, although late and crowded. I had gone from knickers to long pants several years before. I was glad to know that others considered me good-natured and easy to get along with.. For the most part I felt my adolescence was pleasant too. Life in general was good, and relaxed.

However, when I was halfway through high school our family suffered three severe blows. The first one was the tragic death of my sister Fannie's husband, Eli Litwiller, on September 5, 1935. When I was a little boy in Illinois and stood on a chair at the kitchen table to see what was going on across the road, Eli was the one I watched when he was breaking in the horses. He was the one with the jovial chuckle and we enjoyed how he could wiggle his ears and use his forehead muscles to make his hair stand on end. This family stayed behind in Illinois and now had eight children, the youngest one nine months old.

The roads in their community were being graveled and Eli was making extra money with his old dump truck. He would haul a load of gravel and dump it against a previous load on the road. He had saved enough money that he could now get rid of the dump truck and buy a tractor. He was on the way to complete the transaction, with his savings in his wallet, when he came to the railroad crossing. The banks were steep and close enough together so that visibility was poor. As he crossed the tracks he was struck by the unexpected train. His car was completely demolished and his body mutilated. The train stopped and the crew and others got out to survey the accident scene. They called local officials who came promptly and opened the wallet for identification. Of course there was no money there by then. Someone had taken it and the savings were beyond recovery.

We sad Indiana relatives went to the funeral which was very large. We were told what a challenge the undertaker had had in preparing the body for the casket and viewing. He had asked for a picture and the only one available was the wedding picture, but he had done his work remarkably well. My sister Fannie was completely overwhelmed and so traumatized that she needed special support. Our sister Carrie had been married a few months before and the young couple came at once to help her. Carrie helped her personally and her new husband, Alvin Ebersol, took over the outside work. No wheat would now be sown, but he began to get the implements and livestock ready for a sale. With the help of Eli's brothers, he saw to the sale, the purchase of a house in Hopedale with the proceeds, and getting her settled in the new location in town. She struggled to keep food on the table and eventually had to turn to the government for relief.

The second blow came closer to home that next February. The Bill Litwillers, sister Della's family, were almost ready to move. For several years they had made a deal with the Grasmere Land Company to run a farm on a fifty-fifty basis: they would pay half the expenses and take half the profits. By now they were ready to take on a farm by themselves and had bought a place about thirty miles southeast, near Winamac. They had six children and Della was pregnant with the seventh. Just as everything was quite well lined up for the move Della got sick. Mama went over to help and of course they called the doctor. He told them the fetus was dead and should be removed at once to save her life. She thought it over and decided that rather than hold up the whole proceedings she would risk a week or so and have the operation at the new place where she would have a better time for recovery.

It was a tragic wrong decision. Her condition suddenly became much worse and she died. Again, the funeral was very large and we all felt stunned. Mama brought the children to our house and kept them until the moving was accomplished. Bill had felt they should go ahead and manage as best they could. They kept coming back to the church and to us on most Sundays and thus we could keep in close touch. Bill hired a woman and her son to help him but that did not work out well. As a housekeeper she did not do anything that he could not do and in cooking she just kept opening the cans that Della had prepared. He decided to take over the housekeeping and care of the children himself and hire the farming done. Several years later he married again to Nora Eichelberger and they had a son, Richard. I therefore knew him as a little boy and then we were separated. Years later, when he was in college, we happened to live nearby and would invite him to our home. Thus for a few years the connection was pleasantly renewed.

These deaths were extremely hard on Mama, but she went ahead as always and I had no inkling that she might be tired or aging or weakening in any way. As usual, she and Papa would get up at the same time each morning and as he went to the barn to attend to the stock she would warm up the house and cook the breakfast. Then one morning she did not get up. When Papa went to investigate he found her eyes rather glassy. She said she had a terrific headache, but he could hardly understand what she said. When she couldn't move her arm and leg they knew she had suffered a stroke.

The doctor of course put her on medicines and said she was to drink buttermilk every day. The creamery truck came around every week and so we could keep her supplied. We all rallied around to help what we could. I found myself helping with the dishes and I took her place in milking. Fortunately for us, Minnie was teaching in a nearby school and was boarding at home. She therefore took over the housekeeping, especially on Saturdays. Lydia lived a mile away and came every week to do the laundry. Grandpa Miller moved over to the Reinhardt home.

At that time there were no programs available for rehabilitation, but Mama made up her own program. She was so determined to regain certain movements and to improve her speech that after ten days or so in bed she tried to get up and see what she could do. The doctor had told her she needed to have her teeth pulled. To improve enough to go through that ordeal and recover from it would clearly take a long time in itself and we all prepared for a different kind of winter. Day by day she pushed herself along so that she improved steadily, but slowly.

As I was beginning those last two years in high school and taking more responsibility at home I experienced a rather definite turning point in my life. For one thing, I had reached sixteen and could get a driver's license. Now I could take myself wherever I needed to go. I was still bashful and quiet, but I had much more confidence in myself and began to take a more active part in whatever was to be done. For example, on weekdays I would drive Minnie to her school, build up the fire in the school stove, and do any other kind of chores until my school bus would come around. Then I would board the bus for school. In the evenings it would drop me off again at Minnie's school and after we got everything in order to leave the building we would drive home in the car.

Now I could drive to the Literary myself. I did not date anyone as long as I was in high school, but I would pick up a neighbor girl on the way and her cousins would take over her transportation after the Literary. I began to serve on committees, especially the Program Committee. We would meet on Sunday afternoon and decide what the topic should be for the speaker, who should furnish the music, and who should be the critic. The duty of the critic was to make suggestions for both the performers and audience after the program.

Our Sundays were now much quieter. We had fewer guests. I went to church with my parents as usual. My Sunday School class stayed together and we were no longer the Boys' Class, but the Young Men's Class. For some reason we no longer played ball on Sunday afternoons as the class ahead of us did, but the young folks began to gather on Sunday afternoons — almost every week in the summer and about once a month in the winter. We would find out by word of mouth on a Sunday morning at whose home there would be a gathering that day and I often went. Oftener than not, however, I would be playing board games with the Litwiller children at home and Sundays would slip away pleasantly. On Sunday evenings I would now occasionally have to take my turn at an assignment at Young People's Meeting. I would agonize as I prepared my essay, would suffer stage fright when I read it to an audience, and felt no end of relief when it was all over.

I was gaining in strength and experience in farm work just as Papa was aging and needed a lighter load. I enjoyed our working together and he seemed to feel it important that a father should work along with his son. Early in the spring we sowed the oats. While I was in school Papa would disk the corn fields just as soon as the ground allowed. By that time what corn had been left in the fields would have been found by the livestock and other animals. What little was left of the stalks was dried and beaten down. Then we got out the seeder. Papa would drive the team and I, behind him with a scoop shovel, kept pushing the oats into the hoppers at the end of the seeder. The attached fans would then broadcast the seed far and wide.

I especially remember how Papa and I worked together to rebuild our elevator. This was a wooden structure on top of the corn crib that housed the mechanism to bring the corn from the wagon up to the top of the crib and then let the ears fall inside. A very strong wind and hailstorm had blown it down. Fortunately, the metal parts were not damaged but the wooden part had to be restored. Papa was a patient teacher. His temper was rather easily triggered, but he had a keen sense of justice and fairness. When a group of men would be talking together he was likely to be rather quiet, but someone was sure to ask, "Chris, what do *you* think about it?" and he would usually have words of wisdom. I have told before how he was also innovative and he could fix anything.

I had gotten strong enough that I could take a man's place in the harvest. Papa would cut the grain with the binder and he would drop the sheaves in rows to save the shocker some steps. This was my job—to make the shocks. I would pick up two sheaves and set them forcibly together on end for support and then add two more to form the heart of the shock. I would then add about six more or so to make a round shock. I would then spread apart the strawy end of a sheaf, bend the stalks, and place it over the top of the shock. This would give the water a better chance to run off in case of a shower.

By now I could take the team and hayrack to other farms to do our part in the thrashing ring. I would build a good load with the sheaves pitched up to me and then drive my load to the threshing rig and toss the bundles into the machine. I enjoyed those big dinners at noon. The threshers would tease me, saying that when I bent my elbow my mouth would automatically open. I noticed how in an unspoken way we would manage to avoid eating at the home of a very slovenly housekeeper. Somehow we would finish earlier in the forenoon or would not need to begin until afternoon. When a sudden shower might come up we would gather in some shed or cover until it was over. I would enjoy the jovial atmosphere and conversation. Someone might say, "We're all here but the hired man and the dog, and the dog can go under the porch." In our community there were so many Mennonites and Apostolics that the talk never became too coarse or rough. They might discuss President Roosevelt, pro and con, or the Dempsey-Tunney fights, or the scandal among the White Sox going on just then. Several of the dismissed ball players who went to the minor leagues came to Valparaiso and one or two watched our Kouts team at play. Their suggestions probably helped our team reach the championship.

Papa still attended the threshing ring's business meetings, but I knew what was going on. Both meetings were held at the home of the owner of the rig. At the first one it was determined how many farmers needed him and in what order he would work. They decided who needed outside help, how much, and who would fill the need. At the second meeting, held at the end of the season, settlements were made. The thresher would get three cents per bushel that he threshed for wheat and two cents for oats. The work hours were reviewed and if a farmer owed assistance to someone else it was decided how to satisfy the debt. When everything was settled the owner would treat the group to ice cream, a celebration that ended the season. But this important farming event was fast coming to an end. The new combines were arriving in our area and the threshing ring fell apart. Lydia's husband, Ora Gut, bought one and Papa thereafter hired him to cut our wheat also. I thus witnessed the passing of an era in farming.

I would be hot and tired by the end of a summer working day on the farm. Then after supper Papa and I would go outside where it was getting cooler. He had made a hammock that stretched from tree to tree not far from the porch. While he lay in the hammock I would be sprawled nearby on the grass and I thoroughly enjoyed the quiet companionship we could feel as we watched the sunset and our conversation drifted along.

Often Mama would come out on the porch or settle in a chair closer to us. She had lost weight, but she no longer had a slur in her speech and had improved so much that she seemed almost her old self. However, she never regained really good health again. She had to watch her blood pressure the rest of her life. She had had her teeth pulled as the doctor ordered, but she refused dentures. She decided she would rather be limited to soft foods all her days than to go through the difficult experiences her sisters had had with their false teeth. She had to curtail her activities and yet could carry on most of her housekeeping again.

I realized more than ever before what she had gone through in her life—how she cooked and baked, canned and mended for a large family. She managed a large truck patch and garden and helped in the fields when especially needed. Sick neighbors could count on her for help and also when they had new babies. She nursed us all through our childhood diseases. She was a gentle, good-natured person, often doing without something for the sake of the rest of us. My sisters said she had never had a good stove for her cooking skills until in 1913 she got the Home Comfort Range she so highly prized. I too appreciated that old stove that produced so many good things for us, and I never knew another stove in our kitchen.

As we three consistently watched the dark come on, listened to the cicadas and bull frogs, enjoyed the lightning bugs at play, and engaged in quiet conversation of all kinds, I realized afresh what special parents I had. They had endured so much, appreciating life's joys and accepting its sorrows. We experienced a closeness that seemed like a special benediction. I had my parents all to myself, a rare experience in a large family. I was so fortunate to have them and they seemed glad to have a son still around that had been so close to death three different times. As long as I have my mind I'll cherish the memories of those summer evenings with my parents.

I was back in school when it was time to harvest the corn in the fall. That was something most of the farmers in the neighborhood would not have tolerated, and even the boys would have wanted to drop out of school at age sixteen. My parents, on the other hand, encouraged our going on in school as far as we could. (Unfortunately, my oldest sisters had had no way to get to high school in Illinois.)

Because of family circumstances Papa was not able to finish high school, but he was a progressive farmer who kept up with agricultural bulletins and farm magazines. I did not realize until later how Papa reflected his Illinois background in raising corn and hogs. In normal times we sold about fifty pigs a year and two-thirds of our fields were given to corn, a contrast to the more diversified farming typical in northern Indiana. Corn was a special business for us—the planting, the cultivating of the long rows through the summer, and now the husking (we called it shucking) in the fall.

Without a silo we resorted to the usual way of harvesting corn. Due to the depression Papa could no longer hire help for the shucking, and so Mama was the one to pick up a husking peg and help shuck the ears from the stalks and toss them into the wagon. I would help as much as I could after school and on Saturdays to bring the corn to the crib where in the next months it would dry out completely, or as completely as a wet season would allow. The time to shell it and take it to market was in February, when the kernels were hard and dry and the prices were more favorable.

We no longer rented the usual shelling machine, drawn up beside the crib and run by tractor power, for Matt Heinold had invented a one-man sheller by mounting it on his powerful old truck and running it by truck power. In the exchange of labor, Papa would inform several of the neighbors when he would be ready to shell corn. They would come at the appointed time and two or more openings would be made in the side of the crib. With special rake-like forks, supplied by Matt, they raked out the corn onto a wide belt that carried the ears up to the sheller. There, with considerable noise, the shelled corn dropped into a tube or chute that carried it into a wagon while the cobs flew out in another direction. As the men reached the lower layers of corn in the crib the rats began to dash out, trying hard to scamper away before being clubbed. They usually lost.

We never wasted anything that could have a possible use. We gathered the cobs and stored them in the cob house (woodhouse). They and any thoroughly moldy ears would make good fuel for our stoves. Often bits of husk had persistently clung to an ear, but in the shelling process would fly away and eventually they accumulated into quite a little heap. These also had a use. When we threshed grain in the summer we would fill our mattresses with fresh clean straw. Even though we would have feather ticks over the mattresses, they would be considerably flattened by February. Mama would open the mattresses and stuff these soft husks into the straw. Our beds would be higher than usual for a time, but the flattening process would begin again.

One day when the shelling was going on a team of two women from the Jehovah's Witnesses, sent out to distribute tracts, happened by and stopped in to watch the process. When they noticed the pile of fresh red cobs they asked whether they might have some to make corn syrup. They of course could have as many as they wished. Mama was interested in this and found out how to make it. She filled a huge kettle with clean fresh cobs and boiled them until the water took on the color of strong tea. She then drained off the liquid, added the suggested amount of sugar and sure enough, when it was cooled down she had several gallons of corn syrup! This was one of the things, however, that she could not keep up.

The last two years of high school were much more interesting and challenging for me. In our whole school about fifteen out of eighty students were Mennonite. Now as juniors, because of the drop-outs, there were only three of us in a class of sixteen. With our class so small and our teachers really interested in our getting as much education as they could provide, our relationships became closer and more meaningful. We all felt well acquainted and friendly, and learning was important.

Our principal, Mr. Charles McMurtry, took the boys of our class and Mary Kosanke and Lilah Schwanke, the two brightest girls, and formed a geometry class. He said we might find it useful as such if we had anything to do with architecture, but his purpose was to teach us to think and solve problems. We began with plane geometry and at the end of the semester he entered us into a state contest. We had no special preparation—we simply took a test, and we tied for first place. The next semester we studied solid geometry and this time took first place all by ourselves!

As to history, by the time we graduated we had been exposed to ancient, medieval, United States, and modern history, while constantly paying attention to current events. We also were offered practical courses like commercial law, salesmanship, and bookkeeping. Miss Dittmer, our English teacher, was conscientious about grading our papers, which gave us individual attention. Our grade cards came out every six weeks. Within that unit she would have us write a major paper, stressing the organization of our thoughts, and she taught us how to use footnotes. She also had us diagram sentences. Her classes, along with my Latin, gave me a deeper appreciation and so much more knowledge of our own English language as to vocabulary, structure, and usage.

She also taught our class in government and civics. The special memory I have of that class is how she assigned Paul Vogel, the smartest boy in the class, and me to a debate. The question was: "Resolved, that a certain sum of money is better spent on physical fitness than on a battleship." Paul had the affirmative and I was to argue the negative, which was completely opposite from what I believed. I floundered around, wondering what I could possibly say. I started with the Greek concept of well-being, "a sound mind in a sound body." To achieve this you couldn't just deal with the abstract—you had to deal with specifics: training, regulations, and equipment to build physical fitness, as you would for a battleship. I didn't think I made a good case, but I was pleased that I got more applause than Paul did! Not until later did it occur to me that Miss Dittmer had probably chosen us two deliberately to make us think. She knew I was a Mennonite and no doubt thought I should give my pacifist position more thought.

Mr. McMurtry also arranged field trips so that we could see more of the outside world. I especially remember how he took a load of us boys to John Deere Day, when farmers got together to hear new ideas and see new equipment. There were speeches and demonstrations, movies and exhibits. We could take part in the drawing and enjoy the eats. It was such an enjoyable day. I was sure I was going to be a farmer.

Mr. McMurtry also took us to a steel mill in Gary and we stopped in at a bakery to see how Wonder Bread was made. We also spent a day at Valparaiso University. We could get an idea of the campus and classroom atmosphere, and we ate in the cafeteria. Some of us boys paid a visit to the physics lab and I especially remember the wind tunnel there that they used for testing purposes. At the end of an interesting day we attended a basketball game. That was an exciting experience for us, as we had no gym at Kouts and we never had seen a basketball game played on a college level.

Back at school we senior fellows would cross the street every day to see how the building of the new school was progressing. Year by year the trustees had laid aside a certain sum for a new school and now there was enough saved that the Government was willing to supply the rest. We saw the WPA (Works Progress Administration) at its best. Local men who really needed extra income were working industriously with a sense of community purpose and accomplishment. It gave us a very positive feeling about the future.

As we approached the end of our senior year the days became still more interesting and exciting. There was the matter of choosing class rings. We two Mennonites were not going to order any. We were surprised that out of deference to us they decided to order sweaters instead. Our class colors were crimson and white. We therefore got crimson sweaters with white emblems in front. We liked our sweaters, but they turned out to be too warm to be worn just anywhere.

The time came for the senior play. Miss Dittmer found a play with thirteen parts entitled "Cheerio, My Deario," but this meant that two of us had to share the part of the black porter. I appeared in the part one night and another fellow the other night. We could do some practicing and learning of parts during class time. When Miss Dittmer was blackening me for the performance she chuckled. When I wondered what was so funny, she said, "Oh, I just had to laugh at that long black neck."

Near the end of the school year we observed a Senior Day. We all gathered at our usual places in the Assembly Hall, the freshmen along one side, the sophomores next, then the juniors, and we seniors along the other wall. This was the time when the honors and awards were announced for the athletes and other departments. Paul Vogel and Mary Kosanke were named as co-valedictorians and Lilah Schwanke was salutatorian. Mr. McMurtry then gave a little speech about our sailing on a ship. As older sailors moved on, younger sailors were taking their places and the ship would sail on. He then introduced each senior and as he called our names we were to come forward and make some remarks. When it was my turn I said I was not leaving the old ship like a rat that knows when it is no longer seaworthy and that it will sink, but the sailors coming on would be going on as before on a new ship, the new school building.

At the very end of the year we had the Senior Dinner. It was catered in the hall across the street and was attended not only by the seniors, but also the teachers and perhaps the juniors. (My memory of this occasion is vague.) The Senior Dinner had been dropped during the Depression but Miss Dittmer, our class sponsor, thought it was time to reestablish it. I enjoyed the food, but all I remember about it is what they called "mock chicken." Something like a sucker-sticker was pushed into some kind of meat. It was good, but I don't know what it was.

I was interested in the program while we sat at our tables after our meal, but the details of the class history, class will, and class prophecy have all escaped my memory, except one detail. The prophecy said I would be a Stepin Fetchit. I grinned because the others were enjoying the idea, but I didn't know what they were talking about. Fortunately, I was sitting beside Mr. McMurtry who quietly explained that Stepin Fetchit was a black movie star who could dance very well. When the music started and things were being cleared for the dancing, James — the other Mennonite boy — and I and one other fellow slipped away. To give ourselves a final treat we drove to Valparaiso and had ice cream.

Papa had come alone to the senior play, but now at graduation both of my parents came. Commencement was held at the Christian Church. The setting was simple and quite ordinary, but the graduates dressed up for this special occasion. We fellows wore gray suits and the girls wore white dresses. In consideration for the girl that was pregnant, they all chose a pattern with a loose jacket. As I recall, we all wore white shoes The girls had corsages of gardenias and we boys each wore a gardenia boutonnière in our lapels. I had never heard of a gardenia until it was chosen as our class flower.

We all sat in a row on the platform along with our principal and the speaker. None of us had any part in the formal portion of the program. Some students from Valparaiso University performed special music. The speaker, the president of some church college I no longer recall, spoke on making choices and their consequences. I remember that he used Samson as an example.

As the program came to an end Mr. McMurtry handed out our diplomas. The speaker followed him down the line, speaking to each one of us quietly. When he came to congratulate me I replied that I hoped when we got out into the world that we could help to make it a better place than what we were experiencing just then. I must have been thinking of our financial struggle, the threat of war at the time and other evils. The speaker looked at me a moment and then said:

> The Lord bless you and keep you.
> The Lord make his face to shine upon you.
> The Lord be gracious unto you, and give you peace.

Fifty years later I received a card from the Kouts Alumni Association inviting me to the alumni banquet at which the Class of 1937 would be especially recognized. I was glad to accept and eager to go. I had not seen my classmates for all these years. Then came a letter from Harold Heinold inviting us all to his home for the noon meal on that day, a time for us to get reacquainted and to reminisce about our school days. I had heard that Harold, a good and steady worker, had established a hog business and when Elsie and I drove up to his lovely country home, we felt he must have been very successful at it.

When we arrived some of my classmates were already there. I was glad to see Paul Vogel, our class president, who was a devout Catholic, a bright and conscientious man. I remembered how Mr. McMurtry was working to get a scholarship for Paul from his own alma mater. Now Paul had several degrees and was researching lubricants, trying to see which one was most effective. Mary Kosanke, the other valedictorian, could not come. She was living in Florida and had pneumonia at the time. Lilah Schwanke, however, was able to come from Oklahoma. Her son was an airline pilot and could make trips possible and easy for her.

I was so surprised to see how Raymond, once our lean and lanky fastest runner in the school, was now so huge, with puffy cheeks. He had served in the war and was now an officer in the Caterpillar Company. Harold had told us how he had sold his hog business to a successor who lowered the standards and exploited the workers. He had felt so disappointed but now was in an investment business that yielded high dividends. When the rest of us were listening with caution I noticed how quickly Raymond could tell Harold that he would invest $2,000 with him.

We were told that Billy, the genial grocery boy, had managed a successful grocery of his own in town but was no longer living. It was sad to find out that James, the other Mennonite in the class, was suffering from Alzheimer's. He could talk a little by telephone when he had had been contacted, but was not at all well enough to come. Always interested in engineering, he had made a good contribution with his skills to the early space program. Barbara sent a message from her home in Ohio to say that her invalid husband was too ill for her to leave him. Two of our girls had married local men and always lived in their home town. It was a real pleasure for me to see that my classmates and their spouses were all good citizens that actually were making their worlds better places.

To my delight Mr. McMurtry showed up in the afternoon. He was now an old man with poor eyesight. He was brought by his daughter who was caring for him in his last days. When it was my chance to talk to him I identified myself and asked whether he remembered me. He said that indeed he did. "And I remember what you said on Senior Day—how you were not leaving the ship like a rat, but with emphasis on the new ship." He told us that in all his career our class had been the most outstanding and special to him. The whole experience in Harold's home was inspiring for me and Mr. McMurtry's visit the crowning point of the trip. I was disappointed not to see Miss Dittmer. She was still living in town and had been invited, but years earlier she had somehow been overlooked or neglected to the point that she lost interest and gave up teaching.

I enjoyed the alumni banquet. We classmates sat together at a special table where we could continue sharing memories, but with less intimacy and many more distractions, so that the evening could not compare with the afternoon. By that time the others knew that I was working for the church, not as a pastor but I was in the office of Mennonite Mutual Aid. I happened to overhear the half-whisper in which one woman said to another, "My! How Clayton has changed!"

Yes, I had changed—in confidence, career, and outlook.

After fifty years one would only expect that, but I did not expect change to come as quickly as it did. At the time I graduated from high school I had no thought but that I would be a farmer and continue the life I was living. Yet at the very time I was receiving my diploma the insurance company that owned our farm was selling it to a man who wanted not only the land, but the use of the farmstead, and we had to leave. The buyer cheerfully told us that he hoped a good war was coming along and he could make a lot of money! Papa investigated several other farms, no doubt thinking of me, but none of them was satisfactory. With Mama in poor health and both of them aging, they decided to buy a seven-acre plot at the edge of Kouts, and the four of us—they, Minnie, and I—moved to town.

I hired out to a neighboring farmer for the summer, but it was not a very satisfactory arrangement. I also was so discouraged, for at a dollar a day I wondered how I could ever accumulate enough to get a farm of my own. Mama was discouraging me from even planning to farm. She reminded me of how the weather and prices were making farming such a gamble and that—after my serious illness of pneumonia—I should not get into the dust and chaff of farm life. At church two different men told Papa that since I now had my education(!) I should go into business and not return to the farm. In my restlessness I knew I would like to go to college. I therefore applied to Valparaiso University but saw at once that there was no way I could afford it.

In my application I had given the name of my minister as a reference. Unbeknownst to me, he tipped off our church school that I was interested in going to college. A representative from Goshen College, located about eighty miles to the east of us, promptly came to see me and confidently showed me how I could work my way through more schooling.

Mama and Papa, 1940

I spent the next three years in Goshen. As a freshman I took a heavy load, especially of science courses, and did janitor work besides. My second year I reduced my course load and took a job on the night shift—from 10:00 to 6:00—in the Goshen Milk Condensery. I was the only one in the plant at night and sometimes the place felt spooky. I did cleaning and would unlock the door for the sugar truck and help load or unload any other trucks that might show up during night hours. In the third year I saw that my draft number would soon be coming up. To reduce my school debt I gave up classes, arranged to board and room with a Weldy family on Eighth Street, and worked at the Condensery full time.

In my first year at college I was of course unusually busy. What little free time I had I hung out with a few other fellows in the dorm who also were quiet and not involved in extracurricular activities. We did not date any girls. I for one had no time or money for dates. My sister Mary, who was now teaching school, thought I should have more of a social life and have dates. When I was not responding, she knew that I was also bashful and pushed even harder. "Why don't you ask Elsie Eash?—She's a good sport."

Actually, I had already noticed Elsie. When we had gone to pick up Mary at college, she brought some of the dorm girls out to the car to make introductions to our family. Elsie was one of them. I could see that she was a lively, friendly person and I found out that she had come to college at age sixteen. She told me long afterward how Mary talked so much about her brother that the girls began to tease her about it. Her retort was, "Aw, you girls are just jealous because you don't have any brothers!"

When Mary kept insisting, I finally found the courage to ask Elsie. I hired a taxi and took her to a concert at the high school. She was such good company and it went so well that it was much easier to ask her again. I became aware of all the events I could take her to right there on campus. We began to get much better acquainted. We told each other our stories. Just as we were getting into a pleasant friendship her father called, asking her to come home to take a school job that had suddenly become available. She felt obligated to take it. As we were saying goodbye I asked whether I might write to her. From that point our friendship really took off.

At Christmas time the next year Elsie made a trip to Goshen to visit her friends. Her parents knew that would include me and they earnestly urged her not to get engaged. I also knew that I had some competition in her home community in Pennsylvania. I stressed to her how much she and I had in common—our friends, our colleges experience, our goals and ideals. She did not agree to become engaged, but she did accept the watch I gave her. As we parted I think we both knew how this friendship would work out.

As I expected, the Government caught up with me and I spent the next three and a half years in the service as a conscientious objector to war (C.O.). When the draft board examined some of us Mennonite men the chairman tried hard to steer us into the noncombatant position. When he saw that we could not be persuaded he gave us no trouble, and we had the added advantage of being members of a "Peace Church." The so-called Peace Churches—Mennonite, Friends (Quaker), and Church of the Brethren (Dunkard)—had organized and worked very hard in Washington, D.C. for recognition of the C.O. position. The negotiations resulted in our being drafted, but we could perform alternative service instead of bearing arms. The Government agreed to supply the camps and declare what would be valid alternative service, but the churches had to bear the expenses, supply the leadership, and take care of the details of camp life. Draft boards who examined C.O.'s who did not belong to Peace Churches gave the fellows a much harder time in testing their sincerity. Some of them were sent to prison as were the "absolutists" who resisted the draft altogether.

I was called up on November 6, 1942, and was assigned to the C.O. camp at Sideling Hill in Pennsylvania, about sixty miles east of where Elsie was teaching. Men kept coming and going at these camps. The camps were in operation about a year before I was drafted and by then had established their structure. The camps were to carry out work of national importance and this one was devoted to soil conservation. I was assigned to go out on the project, but some men were chosen for what we called Overhead—work on the premises to keep the camp running in good order. Some worked in the kitchen or laundry. One fellow had to keep the stoves going in five barracks. Some mowed the grass in season, or shoveled snow. My only part in Overhead was to help wash dishes on weekends and clean out the grease trap. We buried the grease.

We Mennonites and Amish were given booklets written by contemporary Mennonite leaders about Mennonite history, beliefs, and practices. For the first six weeks we had classes based on these booklets, but throughout the year we would be notified about evening meetings for such discussions or visits from church or government officials who came to look in on us. Most of our evenings were free for us to do what we wished, whether to read, listen to the radio, or whatever, but nothing could compare to a weekend leave.

Except for the fire months in spring and fall, we could get a weekend leave once a month. Of course I used mine to go see Elsie. She was teaching at Yoder School, a one-room public school near the Maryland-Pennsylvania line with mostly Amish and Mennonite students and was living with her sister and brother-in-law, Ruth and Alva Yoder. Their farm lay along the Maryland side of the state line. The school that her father had asked her to take earlier, Jack Rager School, was a mountain school near Nanty

Glo, closer to Johnstown. That school was so unruly that the teacher simply walked away mid-term and abandoned the pupils. Elsie was able to demand the respect and discipline that got her through the rest of the year successfully. One pupil was heard to say, "She doesn't spank," and then he added with spirit, "but I bet she could!" Then she was able to transfer to this school which was in an entirely different environment. I was so lucky to discover that one of our unit bosses lived within seven miles of the Yoders and he went home every weekend. For a dollar round trip I could ride to his home, where Alva would meet me on a Friday evening and bring me back on Sunday afternoon.

These visits were the bright spots in the year, but the year was a very hard one for me. I was in such a strange environment and was homesick. I was working, but not getting anywhere, and my efforts were so futile. I felt I wasn't even doing anything for my country, for our work along the Turnpike seemed like make-work to keep us busy. The conscientious objectors were generally misunderstood and in many cases mistreated because they were considered unpatriotic and disloyal. The community around Sideling Hill was not as hostile to the campers as in many places, but we fellows were encouraged not to hang around in the nearby village of Wells Tannery and be conspicuous. I wanted to marry Elsie but I couldn't plan for any future with her when I was getting only two dollars and a half a month! When the camps first started the Mennonite Central Committee gave the boys five dollars a month spending money, but the camp program was getting so big and expensive that they had to cut the allowance in half by my time.

One day when I not only felt emotionally upset, but wasn't feeling well physically, I started walking out of camp on a narrow dirt road that had high banks of shale on both sides where nothing grew. Finally I climbed one of those banks and threw myself down on the shale in utter despair. I can't remember any time in my life when I was at a lower ebb, but it turned out to be a most significant turning point.

As I lay there a strange calmness began to steal over me. Whether due to the model of my parents, the influence of my church, or growing maturity, I only know that something reminded me that the Christian never believed that he was so completely self-sufficient that he could manage every experience or "conquer every foe." There was something higher and beyond our comprehension that gave us meaning to carry on and the strength to do it. As I think back to this experience, it seemed as though the self-part of me was yielding to the soul-part of me. In church language, I was learning to "cast my burden" of what I could not control "on the Lord." I realized that I must go on in faith and trust, step by step, doing the best I could with each step and then just "rest in the Lord" and carry on. With a new sense of purpose and perspective I got up and walked back to camp.

From then on I seemed to find my place in the whole scheme of things. I appreciated very much the fortunate things that came my way. I was working with fencing on a farm especially connected with soil conservation. A huge Amishman was assigned to cut fence posts in the nearby woods and he was told he could choose an assistant. I was pleased that he chose me. He was such a genial fellow and we had a good time working together. It seemed I was learning how to make comrades out of the fellows around me and I enjoyed the evenings more. Of the various things one could do, many chose some kind of crafts, and I took to rug-making. There also were board games and sports. For example, each dorm had a basketball team. If one didn't join a team, he could enjoy watching the competition. And I had such good news from home: the Kouts church had decided to send each of their C.O. boys in service a gift of fifteen dollars a month!

Elsie and I decided to get married and simply do the best we could under whatever circumstances were ahead of us. I had a leave coming up on Friday, October 8, 1943, which we chose for our wedding. The director of our camp was a young Mennonite minster, Sanford Shetler. I asked him to officiate and I asked two of my camp friends, Arthur Weaver and John Martin, to be my best man and usher. Elsie taught the full school day that Friday, but she said later that she wondered what she actually managed to teach that day!

October 8, 1943

We would be married in Springs Mennonite Church, Elsie's sister Ruth's family church, on the Pennsylvania side of the line. The Mennonite community stretched across both sides and Elsie invited her many friends from both school and church. The church was filled that evening, the men sitting on one side and the women the other. We four, however — Art and I and Elsie and her sister Esther sat together in the front. After a usual church service of hymns, Scripture, prayers, and a short sermon, we four rose, Elsie and I repeated our vows, and then we couples came down the main aisle to the back doors. We took our places there and the congregation filed by with friendly, hearty congratulations. After the rice was thrown, Elsie's brother-in-law (Florence's husband, Charles Thomas) whisked us away to the local hotel.

The next day we had our pictures taken and then took a bus to Elsie's home near Johnstown. On Sunday the wedding party came together again for the wedding feast at noon. It was a typical ample Pennsylvania Dutch Sunday dinner, but there was no fancy, decorated cake. It was a joyous occasion. After our farewells, by evening Elsie and I were back at our separate posts, ready to undertake the usual day's work.

At the end of my second year the government closed our camp, which had been built for the Civilian Conservation Corps under President Roosevelt. Now it was to be used for German prisoners of war. We each were asked what other camp we would prefer. About twenty of us had been together for many months and hoped to stay together. We knew the others would prefer camps near their homes, and so we chose one farthest away — in California! The plan worked and a train was soon carrying us across the country to Camino which was in the Sacramento area, but the forestry camp was a little more remote.

I was assigned to assist the nurse in the hospital, a small five-bed infirmary located in one of the barracks farther out. I was a kind of errand boy, doing the cleaning and carrying trays. The nurse was so homesick for her Filipino boyfriend in Chicago that she began to teach me everything she could so that I could take her place. In a month she was gone, but by then I knew how to do throat swabs and backrubs and what to do for fevers and bad colds. As far as I know, everything was going well, but I was alone most of the time.

The National Service Board for Religious Objectors (NSBRO) was the office in Washington, DC, for us C.O.'s. They put out a monthly newsletter for us known as *The Reporter*. One day when I was reading the latest issue I saw an announcement that grabbed my attention. The government was asking for C.O. volunteers willing to be inoculated with several kinds of pneumonia in connection with a study carried on with Fort Bragg in North Carolina. I promptly applied and was accepted. Thus, after nine months in California, I found myself crossing the country again by train, but this time the wartime travel was more difficult. I was not riding Pullman as we had the first time, but for five days sat squeezed into a crowded seat. By the time I reached Pinehurst, North Carolina, my feet were severely swollen.

The government had rented an old hotel in Pinehurst and put thirty of us volunteers in separate rooms to be isolated from the public. The only way we could socialize with anyone was to open our windows and stick our heads out to carry on a little camaraderie with the other volunteers. The men who had been volunteers ahead of us now brought us our food, took our laundry, and ran any necessary errands. Doctors and nurses checked us every day as to fevers, blood pressure, or x-rays. Even so, we had so much time to ourselves. I did a lot of reading, took a correspondence course in agricultural bookkeeping, and wrote to Elsie.

In three months our part of the study was finished. We were asked whether we wanted to return to camp or work in a mental hospital. I chose the hospital and was assigned to Spring Grove State Hospital in Catonsville, Maryland, a suburb of Baltimore. The war was dragging on and the strain of separation was getting ever greater for Elsie and me. Like the soldiers' wives who tried to find work closer to where their husbands were stationed, many CPS wives also tried to cut down the distances. In our case a summer job was even available in the same institution. Elsie accepted it and we could live in a government apartment until she returned to her school job in the fall of 1945.

First I was given a week's vacation and we used it to see our parents. We travelled by bus to Kouts to see my family and then went to Johnstown in the last half of the week. Time passed so soon and we had to report to work. As we were leaving we noticed a few unusual pimples on my skin. Elsie's mother said it reminded her of chicken pox. That seemed so unlikely that we didn't take it seriously. The bus was so crowded that I had to stand all the way to Baltimore. As it swayed and swerved through the mountains and the cigarette smoke got heavier and heavier, I found myself getting sick. I had nausea and a severe headache and by the time we reached our destination I had broken out! Representatives from CPS met us. They had planned a nice reception for the newcomers and had an apartment ready for us, but I was so miserable that I was immediately put to bed and quarantined for several weeks. Elsie went to work on the women's ward and the other transfers were assigned to specific men's wards. I never knew what our wages were to be, for the government withheld all but $15 a month since we were conscientious objectors. The understanding had been that the pooled sum would be for humanitarian purposes rather than for the war. In spite of pleas from our representatives we think the money was simply funneled to the general funds and that we had no control whatever as to how it was used.

When I was ready for work I became an assistant to work on a rotating basis on all six wards. Thus I could get acquainted with the attendants and learn to know practically all the inmates, as well as get familiar with the work and concerns and yet not have to make the major decisions. My shift was from six to six and therefore our earliest task was to pass out the clothes which the laundry brought in. This was done wholesale, as the suits and underwear were all alike. The better patients, glad for something to do, helped with this as well as helping to see to it that the men shaved and bathed in the adjoining bathroom and got to the dining room on time, where they mostly ate with their fingers.

Each ward had about seventy or eighty men. The room was large with beds and benches around the edges. These were not the violent wards and we were never threatened, but we had to be alert every minute. There was always a hum of conversation going on and sometimes we had to diffuse the anger in a dispute or calm an excited person. We would help the doctors give shock treatments and take note of appointments. Sometimes men with musical talent could be transferred to a group that was practicing or performing. We were on our feet most of the time but when the room seemed calm enough we could slip into an adjoining alcove and sit for a few minutes.

Unfortunately, the men had so little to do, which was hard on everybody. In some hospitals the situation was really grim. It gives me satisfaction to know that our CPS men were the ones who revealed the conditions to the public and started a movement all over the country to improve the lot of the mentally ill. Because of their reports and concerns the Mennonites themselves established several hospitals with high standards.

The war ended in Europe. We hoped we could be released soon, for some soldiers were being discharged. Then in August the terrible bombs were dropped in Japan and the war was declared over. Elsie was the only attendant working in the women's ward the evening of V-J Day, August 15, 1945, when the Japanese surrendered. When some of the patients heard the noise of celebrations outside they became very agitated, thinking that Baltimore was being attacked. The C.O.'s had to wait to be discharged until the soldiers were taken care of, but the next spring I was released. I can't remember the exact date when I received my discharge papers, but it was on Good Friday[4] in 1946. I hastily packed my belongings and hurried away to the Yoder farm to be with Elsie.

I could see that there would be no job available in this community. While I was wondering what to do when Elsie's school year was over, I helped Alva with fencing and as many chores as I could. Elsie and I had agreed to go into the service of the Mennonite Board of Missions and Charities at some time. The Board had contacted men when we were still at Sideling Hill and I made a commitment for myself at that time. Now, however, there did not seem to be any place for that.

Those weeks of feeling unsettled were soon interrupted by a call from my sister Minnie. She said that Mama's congestive heart failure was so serious that she was failing fast—would I come home? I hurried to Kouts and found that there had already been a week when Mama had hardly talked. She found it difficult to breathe when she was lying down, but she wasn't strong enough to be up and around. She was living in her recliner chair. I was there about a week when the minister came to see her. We were all together when he led devotions with Mama. After he left she said, "Oh, I feel so refreshed. I think I'd like to go to bed now." But she went into a coma. We sat up with her all night and in the morning she passed away, with Papa holding her hand.

She died on June 7, 1946, the last day of Elsie's school year. Elsie packed all her possessions, preparing to live together permanently and arrived in time for the funeral which was large, as expected. Papa couldn't bring himself to help with any of the arrangements. We four local children—Lawrence, Lydia, Minnie, and I—did the best we could to attend to everything. I'll never forget how Mama's sisters, with their arms around one another, grieved beside her casket.

---

[4] April 4, 1946

Mama's death had a profound effect on us all, but life had to go on. Elsie helped Minnie with the housekeeping and gardening. I was fortunate to get a job working with Papa. He had been hired to remodel the Heinold grain elevator in nearby Aylesworth and I was so pleased to be hired as his assistant.

The Mission Board had not forgotten us. We heard much later that someone had recommended us as good prospects to be in charge of a children's home someday, but there was no such opening. The Board now was asking us to direct the Mennonite Home for the Aged in Eureka, Illinois. Papa went with us to investigate. He was no doubt thinking that he might be living in such a facility sometime, but just now he knew what he would do. Lawrence was moving his family to Florida and wanted Papa to go along to help get settled and build a new house. When we arrived at the Eureka home we found about fifty people in various stages of dependency living in a very large building at the edge of town on a 17-acre plot, but having a farmstead setting. To be responsible for the welfare of fifty people needing individual attention was an enormous challenge to us, but we accepted it.

When we moved in we found the challenge to be even greater than we anticipated. The first year, especially the first month, was particularly difficult because the former superintendent, who was nearing 80 himself and lived nearby, would not give up his authority. He continued to use the office and give directions, considering us to be merely two more helpers, like a cook or laundry woman. To relieve the tension, a Board member from Indiana came and removed all of his things from the office. An agreement was reached that he could be in charge of the farming — the fields, which his son was cultivating, the orchards, and farm animals. Even this was difficult, for when the apples were ripe he took command of all activity and at butchering time he claimed authority in directing the staff when the meat was cut up and packaged in the basement. He put his own meat in the locker as though it belonged to the Home. Only after his son-in-law from Chicago visited — and must have spoken plainly — did he give in and let us assume the responsibility we had been given.

The first thing we did as directors ("superintendent" and "matron") was to raise the wages of the four workers, bringing them up to what we were receiving — fifty dollars a month, plus room and board and the usual household privileges. Thus began the busiest decade in our lives. The day started at 6:00. After the noon meal we had what we called the quiet hour for everyone. That was a good time for me to do business in town or work quietly in my office. We had a "free time" after supper and before the bedtime chores. In the summer we used that time to work in the large garden. We wanted to raise as much produce for the winter as we could. State regulations would not allow canning but Elsie supervised a lot of freezing. She would give an invitation to those residents that felt so inclined to come and help. Therefore there was often a small circle of women, chatting casually as they shelled peas, snapped beans, or peeled apples.

Elsie was an excellent coordinator of the various degrees of attention the members needed. There were always some that were bedfast. Others might be down only temporarily. Those who could get up and out received any needed assistance to get to breakfast. Afterward the staff would take turns in leading the daily devotions. During the usual Sunday morning church time there would always be a staff member on duty so that Elsie and I could frequently attend the Roanoke Mennonite Church. Services for the Home were held on Sunday evenings. Although this was a Mennonite institution, Elsie tried to maintain an ecumenical environment and would invite pastors from other denominations in the community to conduct the services. We used the large living room as our gathering room. We held no funerals there although there were a number of deaths, especially in the cold of winter and the heat of summer. (We had no air conditioning.) The body would be taken away and the funeral would be held in whatever church the person was a member. For those with no church affiliation the funerals would be held in the funeral home and we would take anyone who wanted to attend. There was a long waiting list to get into the Home and we had to get used to the coming and going.

We did not call our residents "inmates" or "patients," but "members," stressing that we were all part of a big family and would live accordingly. The spirit among the members was really quite good. There were naturally little rivalries or disagreements or sensitive feelings. I remember how one member, probably feeling that she ought to have more attention, would claim how much sicker she was than a certain other woman. One morning when she was repeating this again, Elsie had to tell her that the woman had died during the night. The response was, "Oh! but I was so much sicker than she was!"

From the beginning it was my job to fire the furnace! I also did the purchasing, kept the books, ran the errands, handled the emergencies, and made the repairs. The repairs were a much bigger job than I had expected. The building was not in good condition. The roof leaked so much when it rained that we had to run with containers to catch the drips from leaks in the ceilings. To put on a new roof, to do electrical wiring, or repair plumbing, I would call in professional help, but most of the repairs I did myself.

We enjoyed a good relationship with the community. Twice a year women from the neighboring Mennonite churches would come in and give the place a thorough cleaning, including such things as washing the windows and curtains. If nearby farmers had a surplus of produce they would often turn it over to the Home. For years one of our men had strung Christmas lights in great loops along the balcony. When he could no longer do this I took it over. One year I made a huge NOEL spelled out with lights on the front of the building and won the community first prize. I asked our French-born member what Noel meant. He replied, "Good Noose!"

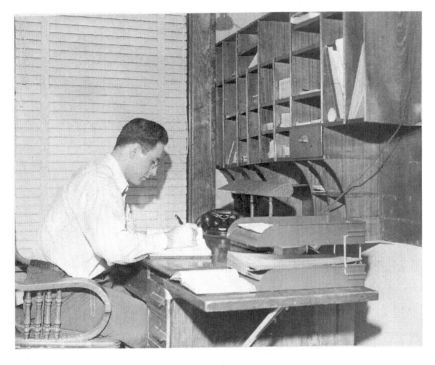

It was easy to get along with our local board that was responsible for the Home. It was composed of five men elected by the Illinois Mennonite Conference from members of the local churches. They met twice a year and we would always keep them informed as to what was going on. They were always cooperative. They seemed satisfied with our reports and gave us free rein.

As the state's standards for nursing homes kept getting higher we were careful to keep our license up to date. We hired a full-time nurse and Elsie and I both took training in practical nursing in Chicago. The state inspectors came twice a year. We were pleased with their remarks when they compared our kind of home to those run for profit. Those directors were more prone to cut corners or to take advantage of their residents.

Meanwhile I was trying to modernize the building as fast as circumstances would permit. I soon had a new heating system installed. Then the coal room, no longer necessary, could be cleaned up and converted into a laundry with modern equipment. In due time we could upgrade the kitchen and I bought a commercial dishwasher and an institutional toaster and we could have a walk-in refrigerator. Every month I sent a financial report to the Mission Board and kept them informed as well as sought their approval for any major changes we wanted to make. One of these was to apply for a Voluntary Service (VS) team to help at the Home.

Stirred by the example of the CPS men doing alternative service for their country instead of bearing arms, many young people, especially young women at first, wanted to show their loyalty to their country by responding to needs through their church as people of peace. The Mennonite Central Committee harnessed and organized this energy and idealism by forming VS units to serve sacrificially for specific terms in cases of need. I thought our Home could qualify, but the supervisor of the units turned me down saying the work would not be evangelistic enough!

It happened that a nonreligious couple had been living in the home when the wife became very ill. Caring for her was very difficult and demanding, but Elsie conscientiously gave of herself as far as possible to do what she could. After the woman's death her husband declared he wanted to be baptized and become a Christian. He said that when he observed what kind of love and attention someone like Elsie would give to his wife he wanted to live that kind of a life too. Someone carried the story to the VS supervisor saying, "If leading someone into the Christian faith isn't evangelism, then I'd like to know what is!" The supervisor changed his mind and we had the help of two girls for six weeks. We had more units later on. After the war when Selective Service classified C.O. men as "I-W" we were able to have one or two at a time in two-year alternative service assignments. They could help care for the men inside and perform a variety of tasks outside on the grounds and with the farm animals.

Through the Mission Board I was able to enlarge my experience and my vision for my job. I found that various denominations had organized a national Protestant Home and Hospital Association which held a convention every year. The Mission Board would send us directors to those meetings. There I would meet the other Mennonite directors and enjoyed getting acquainted and sharing ideas and experiences. At one of those conventions held in Chicago our leader, Ernest Bennett, called us to his hotel room to discuss whether we should organize on our own. He and Herman Andres, head of the Bethel Deaconess Home and Hospital in Kansas, felt confident that we were strong enough to go ahead. Therefore in 1952 I saw the very beginning of one of our Mennonite organizations, the Association of Mennonite Hospitals and Homes.

A new situation arose at the Home when Mrs. Emma Finger, the elderly widow next door, proposed that she would donate her house and land to the Home if we would be willing to care for her and her blind son as long as they needed it. This proposal was not difficult to accept and I did the legal work through a lawyer in town. Of course the process also involved the local Board which took over responsibility for the land—her twenty acres adjoining our seventeen and the forty acres about eight miles away that she also owned. Her death occurred only six months later and the son moved to the Home. When the house was cleared our own family moved into it in 1953 (we had been living in very small quarters inside the Home) and we could use some of the upstairs rooms for the Voluntary Service girls.

Another major change occurred in 1955 when a woman asked to build a little house on our grounds which she would give to the Home when she could no longer live there. This too was managed successfully and the builders designed an appropriate little house. None of us realized how significantly this venture would develop for the Home in the years to come. There are now over one hundred cottages at what has come to be called Maple Lawn Homes.

During this decade in Illinois our four children were born—Sem Christian, named for his grandfathers, in 1948; Miriam in 1951; Beth in 1954; and Ruth in 1955. They were lively, interesting youngsters and well-acquainted with the Home's members, especially Sem and Miriam, who played and romped throughout the building. A VS girl attended to the smaller ones. They were growing fast and we felt they should have more individual parental attention than we could give them in an institutional setting.   That would mean moving on to something different somewhere else.   We thought it over and handed in our resignation in February of 1956, but the Mission Board could not find a replacement until October.

Then we moved to Goshen, Indiana. We bought a house on Eleventh Street and easily made a home for ourselves and entered into community life. We joined the East Goshen Mennonite Church. The children appreciated the closeness of our family life and enjoyed play in the church, neighborhood, and school. Sem and Miriam missed the old folks and an older childless couple in the church took special interest in them and their little sisters. To the satisfaction of both sides this couple became Grandpa and Grandma Hartzler.

I needed a job at once to support my family and was glad to find work with the Menno Travel Service.   This office and that of another young Mennonite organization, Mennonite Mutual Aid (MMA) shared space in what had once been a residence on Eighth Street.   The front room was occupied by the secretaries who directed inquiries to the right place. My office was in what had been the dining room. The desks in back were given to MMA. The travel service had begun just after the war. As the CPS men shifted from one location to another and as less experienced young people entered VS the Mennonite Central Committee created this agency for the sake of efficiency and convenience as well as aid and confidence for the young travelers. Soon this service was available to anyone who wanted it. I found myself planning itineraries, booking tickets, and making many long distance calls.

MMA also grew out of Mennonite Central Committee, which had been a response to the disruptions, problems and great needs after World War I and the Russian Revolution. It had always been a practice of Mennonites to help one another in need – "to bear one another's burdens." After World War II came a special challenge as the CPS men came home and wanted to follow a vocation or build a career of their own. So often they needed more help than their families or churches could give them. They had no credit but needed loans for a car, house, or further training. A young man from Iowa, Harold Swartzendruber, allergic to the grains in his family's milling business, worked in the MCC office. His background in shipping grain was useful now as a huge volume of relief supplies needed to be shipped abroad. One step led to the next and he now was a leader in MMA and in charge of the Goshen office. The MMA was growing so fast that the desks had a little more than they could handle. Since I had time for it, I was given some overflow assignments in auto insurance. Meanwhile some men in our congregation had established Officecar, a bookkeeping and tax preparation company. I was not finding travel planning very interesting, so when they invited me to join them I was glad to accept. I enjoyed that work very much.

Meanwhile Elsie was doing volunteer work, especially in the church and school, that fit well in her situation. No doubt that was how people found out what her talents and experience were. At one of the area Mennonite women's meetings she was nominated to be Secretary for Home and Special Interests in the Indiana-Michigan Conference. She was elected and one of her jobs was to give programs to "promote the cause," especially when invited by congregations to speak at Sunday evening services. She would often include our whole family, for example having us sing something appropriate such as "Children of the Heavenly Father."

In our third year in Goshen we got word that Papa had suffered a stroke. Leaving our children in the care of Grandpa and Grandma Hartzler, Elsie and I hurried to Kouts to see how he was and how the family was coping. Papa had been helping Lawrence as long as he was needed, but he liked Florida so well that he would spend his winters there and then he and Minnie would be together in the Kouts home during the summer. His stroke was serious, but light enough that he could rally. However, he needed more care and attention and my sister, Fannie Litwiller, offered to open her home in Hopedale to take care of him. In those last years he had been active, putting cedar siding in the house and cementing the floors of both porches, adding railings. He had dreamed of dividing his seven acres into plots with streets and houses, but he lacked the money. Now with this stroke the dream was forgotten.

In February Papa suffered a really severe stroke which left him in a coma. He died February 27, 1959 at the age of 82. Once again we left the children with the Hartzlers and drove to Illinois for the funeral. A second funeral followed the next day at Kouts, where the burial took place. His death was hard on me. To lose both parents seemed to mark the end of an era. Special family ties had to be loosened and a certain feeling of support was gone.

It happened that one man after another was called away from Officecar so I would be left alone. They urged me to buy the company, but I didn't want to handle it alone and I let it close. I then took a job at the Goshen Sash and Door factory downtown. Later on there was an opening at Hettrick's, a factory making parts for a furniture company in North Carolina. It appealed to me because it was very close to our home and more convenient. Unfortunately, in six months the company went bankrupt and the Goshen plant had to close. I helped with the final disposal of goods and the handling of shipments.

At that very uncertain time we got a call from the Mission Board asking us to become directors at the Old People's Home in Rittman, Ohio, halfway between Wooster and Orrville. I was ready to accept, but the decision was harder on Elsie. We decided to go and arrangements were well underway when our pastor learned about it. We were surprised to find that he felt slighted and thought that he and the congregation should have been consulted.

We found the Rittman Home to be quite different from Eureka. The building was not very large but it was in much better condition. Half of the forty or so residents could manage their own needs quite well. There was no problem about authority, for the former director could hardly wait for retirement. The Home was located next to the Crown Hill Mennonite Church. Although the two were on friendly terms, the church felt no special responsibility for the Home, except that they installed a loud speaker system so that those who did not walk over to the services could listen. We were out in open country and therefore had no community connections of the sort that the Eureka home enjoyed.

A new house was under construction for the new directors, but it was not ready when we arrived and we lived in a trailer for six months. Sem and Miriam were old enough to help in the Home, especially in doing dishes. Now it was the younger girls who made themselves at home with the old folks. Beth became friendly with an old lady who was bedfast and had been rather hard to know. They regularly played childhood games together. One old woodcarver made a pin for a "pretty little nurse" and Beth wore it proudly on her "nurse's cap." One day when Elsie and I were on duty and the children were alone in the new house a terrific hail storm came up and it shattered the storm door. Glass was strewn about and the children were very frightened. "We prayed," Beth said, "but it didn't take."

Our duties were much the same as at Eureka, but the load was not so heavy and at a slower pace. The only major change I needed to make was to install a new sewage system. Once again we could attend a meeting of the Association of Mennonite Hospitals and Homes, this time held in Columbus, Ohio. It marked the merger with the doctors' and nurses' organizations to form a new Mennonite Health Association. Elsie and I enjoyed the break in our activities and I was glad to see my former coworkers again. I particularly remember the earnest conversation that Dorsa Mishler and I had about our work for the church.

While the work at Rittman went along quite smoothly, we found it took a toll on the children, who experienced some difficulties in adjustment to this location. After two years we realized that we needed a situation where we could spend more time with them and we decided to move back to Goshen.

This time we bought a house a mile south of Goshen on the west side of the road leading out of town, State Road 15. This became our real home, the place where the children grew up. With the attached garage transformed into a room, we had a four-bedroom house, all on one floor. The lot was of ordinary size with ample yard space both in front and back. We soon discovered that across the street and hidden behind the trees was the Pine Manor turkey processing plant. The owner hired immigrant workers and housed them in remodeled chicken houses but there was no place for the children to play. When we offered them our yard they happily accepted. They enjoyed the little tree house that was already in the back yard when we bought the property and I made a little drinking fountain beside our house. Ruth and Beth enjoyed their Mexican playmates.

The grade school in Waterford was within walking distance for the younger girls, but Miriam—now in seventh grade—rode the bus to the middle school west of town. Sem had begun high school in Ohio and there was a Mennonite high school (Bethany) within walking distance on our road, but he had already become interested in the Classics and had begun to study Latin. Bethany did not offer Latin and he chose Goshen High School in town, also riding a bus to get there. When the girls were ready for high school Miriam and Ruth chose Bethany because they had friends attending there. Beth chose Goshen High, I suppose for the same reason. Elsie and I would faithfully attend the PTA meetings and the children's programs, but there did not seem to be as many then as there are now, and Sem was not on the ball teams.

When we returned to Goshen I again needed to find work at once and I naturally turned to Mennonite Mutual Aid (MMA) as a possibility. Both Menno Travel and MMA had grown rapidly and they now shared space in a new brick building between Goshen College and Goshen General Hospital. They had hired more staff and there was no appropriate opening for me at the time. The college was in the midst of building new dormitories and I was fortunate to get a job in construction there. Several years later Harold Swartzendruber offered me a job as a field worker for MMA, but the children were still so young that we felt I should not be on the road and away from them that much.

When Ruth was in first grade Elsie thought about going back to teaching school. We held a family council meeting to consider it. The children approved of the idea and were willing to assume part of the household work that needed to be shared. Elsie's first job was to complete a term in a country school east of Goshen run by a conservative Mennonite community (Clinton Christian Day School). Her teaching skills were soon recognized and the next year she was hired to teach in the public Clinton Community

School nearby. Now all six of us were away from home all day. The others would have their lunch provided at their schools, but I packed and carried my lunch every day.

The children got home first. Elsie was very good at organizing activities. I remember that Sem and Miriam were expected to have supper prepared. I would get home last of all. As time went on a typical weekday evening would find the children doing their homework, Elsie making lesson plans and grading papers, and I would be repairing something. I was the "fixer" if there was something to be fixed. If someone had a special assignment, especially a hard one, she would tell us about it and we would all take special interest, offering suggestions or even helping if appropriate. In the summer there were jobs to share outside. I remember that when I was fertilizing the lawn the children, half joking, complained—why make the grass grow longer and faster and more lush when it simply had to be mowed more often?!

Of course we had time for relaxation and recreation. The children had their board games and other diversions. We did not own a TV at that time and our favorite pastime was to read books together, and we did it often. We enjoyed it so much that we looked forward to snow days and free evenings when we could gather round for reading. Elsie chose good books for us and would read to us until her voice gave out and then I would take over. We read several books by Gene Stratton Porter and I especially remember one of the characters in her *Limberlost* books named Freckles.

Another family activity that we enjoyed very much those summers was taking short exploratory trips. For example, when we read about the Limberlost Swamp and found it would be within easy reach of course we wanted to see it. Elsie was teaching fourth-grade Indiana history and could give good suggestions of places of historic or scenic interest, or we might hear of a special festival going on in some town. Thus on these short trips we visited Brown County, the Indian mounds, Bonneyville Mill, James Whitcomb Riley's home, the restored pioneer village at Conner Prairie, and various museums. When we went to visit the Capitol in Indianapolis we knew that the grave of the outlaw John Dillinger was not far away. I had told the children stories about Dillinger and how when I was young at home I watched a gang of rough-looking men speed down the road with a sheriff's car in pursuit and how Dillinger's gang had robbed the bank in nearby San Pierre. They decided they wanted to see his grave, but when we reached the large cemetery the attendant told us he was not allowed to tell us where the grave was. He did, however, more or less indicate a direction, saying that if we kept walking and noted what was around us we might find it. And we did!

Friends who knew how we enjoyed these day trips told us enthusiastically about their experiences camping and highly recommended it. We decided to try it and borrowed a tent. When we put it up the first evening in a state park we happened to be near a number of barbershop quartets apparently preparing for a contest. Their joking and practicing lasted far into the night. We were not only crowded inside the tent, but found it hard to get any sleep with that happy noise outside. The second time we tried it we used a fold-out tent. We enjoyed following the nature trails during the day, but at night we were again uncomfortably crowded and it began to rain, and kept raining. Being so confined and unable to explore our surroundings any further, one of the girls finally exclaimed, "Let's go home!" And that ended our camping experiences. My part in all these happy times was to have the car in shape and full of gas, as well as to pay the fees.

We also took longer trips. About twice a year we would drive to Kouts where two of my sisters were living. When they heard we were coming they would arrange a carry-in meal at one of their homes and we would have a pleasant family reunion. Our children, however, never learned to know their Sutter-Miller cousins very intimately. They were older and our visits were always too short. On the other hand, when we visited Elsie's people in Pennsylvania we would stay a week and our children had a great time playing with their cousins, who were near their own age.

Very often we would extend that trip to get better acquainted with the eastern part of the country. When we made our first visit to Washington, DC with Sem as a small boy one of our relatives and a staff member from the Eureka Home wanted to go along. We took in the usual tourist sites — the Lincoln Memorial, the Mall, the Capitol building, and several museums. The traffic lanes were making driving so difficult for me that I found myself circling around and around, in spite of my "helpful" backseat drivers, until my carload had a lot of fun about how thoroughly we had seen the nation's Capital!

Elsie and I returned to Washington on another trip with the girls in the 1970's. When we were riding the little conveyance that takes the legislators from one building to another in the Senate subway, we saw another one coming toward us. As it came closer someone in our crowd called out, "It's Senator Hartke!" He heard us and as we passed he stood up and waved in the political style.

One summer on our way to visit one of Elsie's college roommates we stopped off to see Lancaster County, Pennsylvania. When we visited the pretzel factory we got to twist some dough into shape ourselves. We were told that the first pretzel shape was made by a monk who copied the prayer pose of arms crossed over the chest. We saw the Ephrata Cloisters and the Lancaster Mennonite Historical Society center as well as the Hans Herr House. This very old cabin reminded us of how early these prosperous, plain-garbed Mennonites had come to America. We also saw the grave of John Sutter in Lititz. He was at the center of the California gold rush. We doubted that we were related, but we had the same name with the same spelling and so we took rubbings from his tombstone.

On our trip to New York City we were fortunate to have Elsie's niece, Phyllis Lehman, who lived there, show us around. She was an excellent guide as we rode the ferry to the Statue of Liberty and also took in a television broadcast where we learned that when the lights came on we were supposed to clap! We learned to be quick getting in and out of the subway trains. Once we were so crowded that one of the girls complained to us later that the passengers were so packed together that she couldn't even bring her head down to a normal position!

One summer we enjoyed a trip to New England. We stayed at tourist homes, as motels were not as common at that time as they are now. I remember seeing the homes of Mark Twain and Louisa

May Alcott and Thoreau's Walden Pond. At Plymouth Rock we saw a replica of the Mayflower and I picked up a pebble to bring home. We climbed Mount Monadnock in New Hampshire, a popular hike because the slope was gradual. Even so, Elsie twisted her ankle and it took one of us on each side to bring her down.

On one of our trips we enjoyed time at a beach on the Atlantic. Once we stopped off to see the Sideling Hill camp where I had spent many months in CPS. Now it was empty and forsaken, but some of the barracks, the director's cabin, and the fellowship hall were still there. German prisoners of war were held there after the CPS men left and they had drawn some pictures on the wall. We also saw three graves of prisoners—on one tombstone the inscription read: "Fritz, a good soldier."

For all of these trips Sem had researched background information and he would fill us in at the various stops. We always read the historical markers and plaques as we went along, making each trip still more interesting and informative. On our way home we would also stop again with the Eashes in Johnstown and I suppose we would give enthusiastic reports of what we had seen.

One thing in our home that continued from our first time in Goshen was Sunday company dinners. Mennonites were used to having company at dinner after church services. We had relatives attending Goshen College, especially Elsie's nieces and nephews (Ruth's and Mable's children) and we would often invite them. We of course had other connections as well and Sunday dinners were a good way to keep in touch. However, we never had as many guests around the table as I had known growing up in Kouts. For one thing our family was smaller and social conditions were different.

One little fellow at church liked to invite himself and he was always welcome. The two Stoltzfus sisters lived near us and often rode home with us. They liked to be invited for dinner for where they boarded there was always roast turkey for dinner and they were tired of it.

One Sunday dinner that I will always remember was when our guests were prisoners from Michigan City. Abe Peters, a

Mennonite minister in our area, became interested in a prison ministry and he would encourage men from our churches to go with him on Saturday evenings when he would meet with a group at the prison. It turned out that his best response came from the men in the East Goshen Church and almost every other week a carload of us would go to Michigan City. We would meet Abe at the prison entrance and he would lead us into a room where a dozen or more men would be brought in by the guards. Abe would usually talk about the Sunday School lesson, but there would be little discussion. On one of those trips that came near Mother's Day the prisoners gave each of us a box of pansies taken from the prison flower beds which we were to take home to our wives.

Eventually we learned that some prisoners were prepared to give a program and had been invited to some churches for Sunday evening meetings. They would not be paid, but the churches were asked to give them a meal before the program. When our church had invited the group and our women were discussing how to handle the dinner Elsie proposed that our family could simply provide the dinner in our home. Three prisoners arrived at our house with two guards who carried their guns in holsters. We had pleasant dinner conversation. One of the men had children and especially enjoyed seeing ours. They seemed to enjoy the food and one of them especially liked the cinnamon-flavored applesauce. When he found out that Ruth had prepared it he paid her special attention and told her that it was so good that he would have to take some of it back in his pocket.

They gave an interesting program. They had made cells out of lightweight material—plywood or perhaps a light metal—which were taller than a man and big enough for a man to be inside them. Three cells were set on the platform and a man took his place in each. Then in their conversation with each other they freely admitted what they had done wrong and how they were punished. When our family was discussing this event later at home we discovered that Ruth was worried about what a mess the applesauce would be in that pocket. When we laughed and told her he never had intended to do it, she cried, "Well how was I to know that he was giving me a compliment?"

Later on we learned that the prison staff had encouraged their talented prisoners to write and perform a program about John the Baptist. Invitations were sent to those of us that had any connection with the prisoners. For some reason Beth was taking Elsie's place in attending the program with me. I remember how it felt when our small group had the door locked behind us before the door in front of us was unlocked and opened. We were an appreciative audience and all of us were greatly impressed with what the prisoners had done. I bought a recording of their performance.

As soon as possible all of us became involved with jobs. When the dormitory project was finished at the College there was no more work for me and I took a job in the plumbing and heating department of the Montgomery Ward store downtown. I am not quite sure how long I worked there, but I remember that I had worked through two Christmases and two year-end inventories when Harold Swartzendruber came to the store to see me. There was an opening at MMA and he was offering me the job! I gladly accepted it. I had been in auto insurance when I worked there before and now I was returning to handle health insurance.

In a short time Elsie too had found her niche. For convenience she wanted to teach in town. Because she was touched by the needs of underprivileged children in North Goshen, she applied for a job in the Chamberlain School. She was accepted and began her long experience there as a skilled and beloved teacher.

Sem found a job stocking shelves, carrying groceries, and cleaning at Evans IGA grocery store. He stayed with it all through high school and college. Along with scholarships he managed his way to graduation from college without accumulating any debt.

As soon as they were old enough the girls began baby-sitting. As Miriam got into high school she was also hired to be in charge of crafts at Camp Amigo in the summer. As a junior at Bethany High School she had a tough learning experience when she was put in charge in charge of the setting and decorations for the junior-senior banquet. A Roman theme had been chosen including such things as togas for the waiters. She arranged for an artificial pond and fountain with appropriate plantings and greenery in such an elaborate style that students wanted their pictures taken in front of the setting. She had worked so hard and been so worried, but she said later that she learned much that served her well the rest of her life. When she was in college she found work with a family living near the Michigan line that catered meals. Soon they established a real restaurant, The Patchwork Quilt, which could give her steady work while training to be a teacher. Her sisters also found work there, but Beth soon found her aching hands could not handle the large bowls of food.

By that time her chronic disease had been diagnosed as rheumatoid arthritis. Her pains started in high school, not long after she had gone through the ordeal of having her wisdom teeth pulled. She was unable to do some of the exercises in her gym class. Her unsympathetic gym teacher insisted that she had to try harder. I do not recall whether this worsened her condition, but in any case an exploratory operation on her knee was recommended to relieve the pain. It was not very helpful. However, with her anti-inflammatory medicines she could have times when she could get along quite normally. In college she found it helpful to use a tape recorder in class rather than try to take notes. For a time she resorted to crutches and unfortunately suffered a fall on the stairs in the Administration Building.

Through those years we attended East Goshen Mennonite Church as a family, for Sem was a day-student in college and although the girls lived in the dormitory we could bring them home for weekends. As the children were growing up they took part in their Sunday School classes, youth groups, and usual youth programs. When the girls were of appropriate age they were part of GMSA, a girls' missionary and service organization.

For several years Elsie was the church librarian, ordering books, introducing them to the congregation, and managing the checkouts. Later she began to teach the preschoolers' Sunday School class. I was involved enough that I became her assistant. While she was telling the Bible stories and teaching the songs I could be gathering the loose ends. I remember one little boy would be happy as long as he could see his mother, but when she would disappear he would cry and cry. But as weeks passed he could finally believe that she would come for him eventually.

(Now he is a counselor at the Oaklawn Mental Health Center!)   I closed milk cartons in a way that made them into building blocks. The youngsters liked to make all kinds of formations with them. As Elsie became better and better acquainted with the families, when she would hear of the arrival of a new baby she would prepare a casserole and we would take it to the home where she would have a prayer for the new child.

In those earlier years before I was an elder I was chosen several times to be one of four visiting leaders. We were each assigned a certain area and were expected to visit every family or single person at least once a quarter as well as to remember birthdays, hospital patients, or any special event in a member's life.   Of course each household or individual was expected to help with the church finances according to their ability or inclination and to help one another whenever a need arose: for example, when the drug problem in Goshen was getting serious. We were so happy that our own children were not tempted, but there were other parents in the church whose children could not resist the exposure and temptation.   The problem was so new and foreign to Mennonites that the Sunday School class of parents our age began to meet on Saturday evenings to discuss the matter and support one another in whatever way was needed.

We had always encouraged our children to be active in worthy causes and to help those in need. Beth and Ruth really responded so heartily — beyond our expectations. While still in grade school they organized a do-good club of some kind. I hope their deeds were well-chosen and skillfully carried out. I only remember that they tried to help a very poor little girl who had a very needy wardrobe.

When the girls were in college they were so touched by the plight of the Mexican farm workers in California that they joined the boycott of lettuce and grapes. When Beth heard about this in Dr. Burkholder's class she pulled aside the lettuce in the cafeteria, explaining to the other students the conditions under which it was grown. Some of the Mennonite Brethren students from California objected, saying that their families grew lettuce and were not guilty of such injustice. This eventually led to an arrangement with Pacific College, the Mennonite Brethren school in California, that Goshen students could study the situation under the guidance of Pacific College and get credit at Goshen. Four students responded from Goshen—Beth, Ruth, and two others. Ruth missed her own graduation from Bethany High School in order to go. We parents were not as enthusiastic as our daughters to have them go that far away at that point in their studies with uncertain results. But their zeal wore us down and we supported the endeavor. I remember Beth telling us about interviewing people on the picket lines, the border patrol, and the farmers, and about studying the differences in culture.

Another example came from Beth's experience in Indianapolis. Beth had decided that she wanted to be an occupational therapist and the best way to do this was to study at Indiana University Indianapolis after two years at Goshen College. She had a professor with whom she became good friends. She told Beth how her sister's husband was so abusive that he was threatening to kill her. It was necessary to move her and her two children to a place where he could not find them.

Knowing that her parents were willing to help people, Beth called us to ask whether we could take in the family for a few days and then pass them on so that they would be hard to trace. This was not an ideal time for us: Elsie had so much back pain that she had to have a substitute at school and she was spending much time in bed. We didn't see how we could say yes, yet in our hesitation we had not given a definite no. To our surprise, the next morning we found the three in a Volkswagen in our driveway! We took care of them until the next Sunday when we took them with us to church and explained their situation to some of our friends. Omer and Dora Troyer volunteered to take them home, understanding that they were to pass them on. However, after several Sundays they were still appearing at church! The Troyers said they enjoyed the little family so much that they didn't want them to leave. They had inquired of Koinonia Farm in Georgia about taking them, but word came back that they were not equipped to do that. The last I heard, they were given refuge at Reba Place in Chicago.

Sem was the first to leave the nest permanently. With a major in history, he graduated from Goshen College in 1970. That spring he married Mabel Amstutz after a long friendship that began in high school. She was the daughter of the college physician and was interested in becoming a doctor herself. They had planned to hold their reception in the Amstutzes' back yard, but the parents discouraged it because of the uncertain weather, so the celebration as well as the ceremony took place at the College Chapel. In the summer the couple left for Chicago where she entered medical school and he satisfied his alternative service requirements before beginning graduate work at the University of Chicago. Their son was born February 5, 1976, the day after his great-grandfather Eash's birthday, but he received the name of his great-grandfather Sutter and his father's middle name: Christian.

Miriam was the next one to leave. In college she met Stephen Lapp from West Liberty, Ohio. By the time they graduated they were engaged and the next August they married in the East Goshen Mennonite Church. They went to his father's farm which in due time became theirs. Like her mother, Miriam was very active in their local church, especially in teaching the children. Also like Elsie, she taught grade school before she had a family and after her three daughters were in school she again returned to teaching. Her mother specialized in fourth grade, but Miriam devoted herself to the third grade.

Beth's health allowed her to finish her training and to take a position as an occupational therapist in Indianapolis. She had been living in the Mennonite House, a large building that served as a home for single men and women who had come to the city for training or employment. There she met Biff Wideman, a non-Mennonite who had graduated from Earlham College, a Quaker school in Richmond, Indiana. When they decided to get married they chose the local Mennonite church for their wedding. Not only our immediate family, but aunts from both sides of the house were able to attend. One feature of the wedding that I especially liked was the yard-long enlarged wedding certificate, worded exactly like the official small one, but in fancy writing. All the wedding guests were invited to sign as witnesses.

Dr. Esther Hodel, whose Smucker family I had known in Illinois, had a son living in the Mennonite House and thus got to know Beth. She saw special potential in the way Beth related to people and encouraged her to get seminary training to enhance her skills. Sometime later Beth received an anonymous $5,000 gift for seminary studies. Although the check came from Koinonia Farm in Georgia, Beth thought she could make a good guess where the gift had come from, although Ernest Hodel said it did not come from his mother. Beth found the natural place to enroll would be the Mennonite seminary in Elkhart, but Biff did not want to go there. Perhaps he thought he would be too submerged in things Mennonite. Her final decision was to attend Bethany, the Church of the Brethren seminary in the suburbs of Chicago. Afterwards she worked at an osteopathic hospital in the city near Sem.

Ruth was in college during the war in Vietnam, a time when people were uneasy and divided—sometimes harshly—in their attitudes about the war and times in general. Ruth heard about the Peace March planned to begin in San Francisco and end in Washington, DC. A corps of about twenty devoted peace advocates began the long walk across the USA to promote peace with their speeches or in any other way that might come up as they proceeded. Ruth was moved to participate and took a bus to St. Louis to join them. Food and lodging would usually be supplied by sympathizers along the way and many people would walk with them for short distances to show support.

When the group came to Elkhart County local peace workers in Elkhart provided their dinner. Elsie and I prepared food for the carry-in meal. We were delighted to meet Ruth and have her sit with us through the evening. When the walkers were assigned to various homes for the night we were glad to take her home with us along with an older minister.

During these years Elsie had become involved in doing many little kindnesses for Emma Blosser Hartzler, a college friend, who had been stricken with polio in 1952 and all of these years was confined to an iron lung and rocking bed. She had known about the Peace Walk and, finding them this close, she expressed a fervent wish to see them. In some way Elsie reported this at the dinner. The marchers were touched and decided to grant her wish. Sure enough, the next day they filed through her room in Goshen where she could see them from her rocking bed and express her support.

I joined the marchers downtown at the intersection of Main Street and US 33 and could show my support by walking with them as far as Benton. In quiet fashion we walked along, two or three abreast, conversing as we went. I was glad that I could walk with Ruth who, I discovered, was called Ruth Truth because she could state her beliefs in such a direct, positive way. Following the walkers was a labeled truck carrying the luggage, first-aid kits, and other necessary supplies. It also had a seat or two for weary walkers that needed short periods of relief. Our guest for the night was not young and we guessed that he used the seat more often than most. At rest stops the marchers would rub one another's feet. Elsie met us at Benton with the car and we had to say goodbye to Ruth. When they reached Washington to witness to the government they carried a coffin halfway up the Capitol steps before they were arrested. They had to spend a night in jail and had a hearing before a judge the next day, but as far as I know they were not fined nor did they suffer any punishment.

Ruth returned home again and in those years when she was not in school she would work in the food services department at Greencroft, the retirement community just east of the College. She had finished four years at Goshen College, but had not completed the requirement for SST, a Study-Service Term in another country. She had once had a Japanese roommate and thought she would like to take a fifth year of college work in Japan. She had a good year at International Christian University located on the outskirts of Tokyo, but was disappointed in only getting to see the former roommate once. Back in Goshen, she was trying to decide what to do next. She had friends in Philadelphia and decided to join them in the hope of finding a job there. After several months she did find work that suited her and her talents very well: she joined the staff of *The Other Side*, a new magazine that was devoted to worthy causes.

Now the home nest was really empty. By then Elsie and I had found our niches and were trying to give our best to our life work: "good measure, pressed down, shaken together, and running over." (Luke 6:38) Elsie was a gifted teacher, not only in the basics of reading and math, but in showing youngsters how school could be interesting and learning could be fun. She was innovative in her methods and ideas. For example, the school building had a classroom with a window especially open to the public and equipped with a sill or shelf that lent itself for displays. The principal wanted Elsie to have that room, for she knew best how to keep creating interesting exhibits.

She could open and enlarge a new world for the children, especially for the disadvantaged or those that had come from isolated places like Appalachia. She might bring the mayor, the chief-of-police, or a man who kept bees to explain their work and concerns. She might take advantage of having a legislator visiting in town to speak to the pupils and she might have them write to their Congressman about some question of public concern.

She used field trips to good advantage. She took the children to a maple sugar camp. She took them to the Oak Ridge and Violett Cemeteries, located at opposite edges of town to show them the names and graves of people who had made various kinds of contributions to Goshen's life and history. She took them to South Bend to see the portage between the St. Joseph and Kankakee Rivers and the Council Oak where the white men made a treaty with the Indians in the seventeenth century.

When they studied eyes she asked the butcher to save beef eyes so that each child had a specimen to examine. She showed them the wonders of Nature. I was never a teacher, but I was indeed a teacher's assistant. I helped gather all kinds of things like turtle eggs and pussy willows not quite open. I had a hobby of collecting interesting little stones and she liked to borrow my "rock collection." For her caterpillars and butterflies I built a cage about eighteen inches wide and thirteen inches high with a solid floor, screened sides, and an overflap door at the side. So that the children had their own places for collections I made each a little six by three-inch cage of mailbox style, their "bug boxes." When someone gave Elsie a group of okra pods I sliced each one open for study. One year a college professor gave Elsie more caterpillars than she expected. The butterflies laid so many eggs that the larvae needed more mulberry leaves than could be handled at school. I found a mulberry tree along the railroad track. Taking an idea from a company in Elkhart that raised butterflies for sale, I tied a huge net over a branch of the tree and released the caterpillars where they would have plenty of leaves to live on.

A number of Elsie's pupils never forgot their favorite teacher. Years later, when they had children of their own, they would bring them for Elsie to see and for them to meet their beloved old teacher. She was interested in them and often had something interesting of Nature to show them. I remember at least three carry-in dinners in her honor after her retirement arranged by the Amish of Clinton Christian School. Even after Elsie was gone a woman who had attended Clinton Community School exclaimed, "She was the best teacher the school ever had!"

I was glad to return to Mennonite Mutual Aid and was determined to do my best. In the beginning I was a kind of correspondent, answering letters, taking phone calls, and directing questions. MMA had grown very substantially from four men and three women (in clerical jobs) to a staff of twenty, most of them more specialized workers. Soon the government established Medicare and Medicaid. Being in health insurance I particularly studied the government's book on Medicare as well as every other source of information I could find until I was considered an expert on Medicare and all questions about it were referred to me.

At about the same time computers were coming into use. The first computer that MMA purchased was about four feet wide, eight or more feet long, and six feet high. Larry Weldy, who had just completed his I-W service, came to us as our computer man who at first punched in the information by hand. It promised to be a tedious job to transfer data from the paper MMA records to the computer and I was assigned the task of making that transition. I designed suitable forms for this shift, filling in the figures in appropriate columns. This was so time-consuming that I began to return to the office after supper and work until ten o'clock. It took me more than a month to complete the transition. At the annual staff banquet that year Larry and I each received a one-hundred-dollar bonus and special recognition for our work.

From the beginning I was in touch with the clients who came to me with their questions and problems and I could really enter into their concerns. I was soon aware that my closest co-worker did not share my interest in people. If there was some question or doubt relating to an MMA regulation he was more concerned with seeing to the business interests of MMA and however he could get MMA through the solution with the least amount of money. I was more interested in the Mennonite ideal of "brother helping brother." I could tell that younger people coming into MMA also felt that some of the regulations should be softened and made more adaptable and at the board meetings professors of economics like Howard Raid (Bluffton) and Carl Kreider (Goshen) agreed. Furthermore, computers were coming into more efficient and adaptable use.

However, Harold Swartzendruber, the director who had been in it from the beginning, was finding change difficult. MMA needed a boost and the Board sent him to Kalamazoo for a year's training to relieve the tension, but when he returned he had not changed his mind. The fact that we had installed a computer seemed to him like enough modernization. I was of two minds. I owed Harold Swartzendruber my job. He and MMA had been so good to me and I was sorry for him to be pushed out. On the other hand I was glad to see the Memo of Understanding revised and the membership enlarged beyond only Amish and Mennonites to include other Anabaptists like the Church of the Brethren, the Apostolics, and the Missionary Church. It was good to bring in more women and give them more responsibility. I had considered it unfair to discriminate in cases of adoption. Since we were helping parents in need when their children were born, I urged aid for needy parents who adopted a child, for they too had expenses. This was arranged later and the money taken from the Sharing Fund. MMA was past its growing pains and doing well.

Although I kept the same desk my work was changing. As one of the oldest workers there I was asked more and more questions. When I could not answer them I directed them to someone who could. Many of them were about discrepancies and complications that I needed to settle. As the questions became more frequent and general I was being called the ombudsman.

In those years I served as an elder in the church. Four elders were chosen on a rotating basis so that each year one would be replaced by a new one. Elders had nothing to do with finances or the institutional part of the church, but with the enrichment of spiritual life and the relationship of members to one another and to the pastor. One thing that I urged was that a woman be elected as elder. Eventually this was done, but it was always an older woman. I kept urging until there were two women as elders, an older one and a younger one. As at work, I was considered a liberal. Many people did not agree with me, and yet were not hostile and slowly agreed.

By then the times had changed in terms of the pastor's position. When I was young pastors supported themselves and served wherever they happened to live. Now Mennonite pastors were receiving more training and more was expected of them. Pastors were paid salaries, evaluated, and voted upon. Congregations assessed their own needs and might give a call to a minister that they felt had special skills to meet them. The minister chose whether or not to accept the call. When we first came to the East Goshen Church they were in transition regarding pastoral salaries, taking an offering the fourth Sunday of the month in partial support. Even when I was still a "visiting brother" and the system of elders had not yet been established, I became involved as preachers came and went. During one of my terms as elder the pastor found it an uneasy and uncomfortable time. Such issues as evaluation or voting for a pastor seemed to him a threat or a downright insult. It was not an easy time for an elder either.

Another innovation coming to our church in those years was the formation of small groups, a practice popular especially in the larger congregations, in order to develop deeper relationships with one another — an opportunity to give one another warmer support, encouragement, or counsel. The groups were to stay small for the sake of building trust and understanding more quickly. The pastor and elders chose some of us couples to get the groups started. The easier part was to place people who suggested like-minded friends who already had much in common. It was harder to place someone who wanted to be in a small group, but was known to have more trouble being satisfied or making friends. Elsie and I had a Christian conviction based on John 6:37 — "He that cometh to me I will in no wise cast out" — and we took anyone with us.

Elsie and I were both absorbed in our vocations, but we enjoyed our avocations very much too. She was always a natural helper to anyone needing it. She did not like committee work, but if someone suffered a misfortune or a great loss, Elsie would be touched by it and would do something appropriately helpful or comforting. She visited people in the hospital and when one of our church women who was working in hospice asked Elsie whether she would be willing to help in that program she readily responded.

I meanwhile was enjoying my gardening and I liked to keep everything around the premises in good repair. Then I rediscovered a hobby interest that had lain dormant for years. The man who was responsible for the layout of our MMA publications took it upon himself to enliven a bare wall in our office hallway. He was a member of the Weavers Guild and one time he put up a display of woven wall hangings which intrigued me. At the same time I noticed an ad in the newspaper announcing that Professor Edna Schantz at the College was going to offer a class in weaving—ten sessions for fifty dollars. I remembered that long ago in CPS camp I had woven a rug as something to do on dull evenings. I had always enjoyed it and now had an impulse to sign up for the weaving class. The class was limited to ten as there were only ten looms available. Miss Schantz led us step by step through the whole process and by the time we had finished I knew I wanted to make myself a loom and take up weaving.

I checked out a book from the public library which told how to put a loom together, but I soon realized that it was too expensive for me in time and money and I should look around for a used loom. I knew that one of the women at MMA was in the Weavers Guild. When I heard that she would be leaving for the year that her husband would be on sabbatical and would not be taking her loom along, I of course asked if I could buy it. She said she couldn't give it up, but since it had to be somewhere while she was away I might borrow it until she wanted it again. I was pleased, and after details and insurance had been taken care of her husband brought the loom to our house. That year showed me how very much I wanted my own loom and for two years I kept looking for a second-hand one.

One day when Miriam called she mentioned that there was a weaver in their community and when we came to visit them I ought to contact him just to watch and talk. I followed her suggestion and had a pleasant visit with him. He referred me to a member of his church that was also a weaver. While I was enjoying this second visit as well, I noticed an unused loom stored off in a corner. When I asked whether he might sell it he said it belonged to his wife who had inherited it and was saving it for their daughter who had shown an interest. Once again I resigned myself to continuing the search.

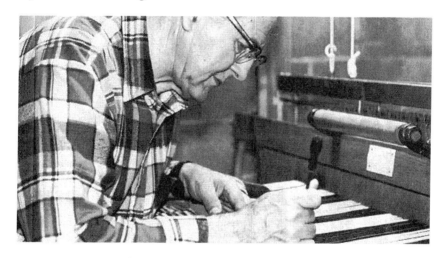

After some months had passed I got a message from this man saying that the daughter had told them to sell the loom, for she could see that her family and involvement in church-planting would keep her too busy to take up weaving. I was glad to buy it but wondered how I would get it from West Liberty, Ohio, to Goshen. I was surprised to learn that they had a son living in Goshen who worked at MMA! They said when they came to see him sometime they would bring it in their truck, but I should have assistance ready to unload it.

When the truck finally arrived I discovered that the loom came in pieces. Unloading it was no longer a problem, but putting it back together would be. Once again I checked out the library book. I eventually got the loom reassembled and everything in running order for weaving. Elsie began to sew together rag strips of various colors and made patterns for me to use. I wove rugs in earnest—not to sell, but to give away: to family members, to the Mennonite Central Committee Relief Sale, for wedding gifts, for any occasion when a rug would be welcome. I thoroughly enjoyed my hobby.

The trip to the Kouts High School alumni reunion came in 1987. It left me in a pleasant glow, but also in a thoughtful mood. There had been fourteen of us graduates: seven boys and seven girls. Two of the fellows were now deceased, but of the remaining five one was a space engineer, another a millionaire hog farmer, one an important officer in the Caterpillar Company, and another with Exxon. I was glad that I could report on a good job, but of course I didn't mention my quiet satisfaction that I was not only making a living, but could help other people feel more secure and contented and even in better health. It gave me real satisfaction to know how well our class had done, a little group from a little country high school. As I thought it over I realized, yes, life was good—I was enjoying so many blessings! Of course, it was not that life had been completely delightful or carefree. Like everybody else in life's journeys we had our heartaches and disappointments. One learning experience was so unexpected and painful that I must mention it in this story.

We were naturally missing our children as they were making their way elsewhere, but in 1978 we were happily looking forward to the possibility that Sem and his little family might move closer again. He was writing his dissertation toward his Ph.D. in history at the University of Chicago and thought he might have future prospects for a position at Goshen College. Mabel was completing her residency requirements for practicing as a pediatrician and had spoken with several doctors in the Goshen-Elkhart area about the possibility of eventually joining their practices. We were already imagining the grandparental relations we could have with little Christian who was two years old.

Then one day we had a call from Sem asking us to come to Chicago—they had something they needed to tell us. We could not imagine what could be on his mind, but we drove to Chicago as soon as we could get free from obligations at home. When we reached their apartment, five floors up in the heart of the city, we found everything normal. We had a pleasant visit and after we cleared everything away from the supper table and Christian was in bed we settled down for serious conversation.

Then they quietly told us that they were separating. When Elsie burst forth with her concern for Christian, Mabel explained to her that he was too young to be upset with the arrangement and they assured us that he would have care and loving attention from both a father and a mother. Sem felt it was the honest thing to go public and he added to our shock and unhappiness by saying that he had a partner and would be living with him.

I was stunned and speechless. Homosexuality was beginning to be talked about openly in those days, but the idea never really registered with me very much, for it was something so far removed from my experience. I had a vague impression from the way people in my background understood the Scriptures that it was a chosen way of life so unnatural, so perverse, that it was downright sinful. Sem explained all about it, saying no one would choose such a lifestyle because of the misunderstanding and mistreatment they knew they would have to endure. He said it might take ten years for us to adjust and accept the situation. He was right. Not until years later did it occur to me what courage it took for him to face his parents, knowing how he had been brought up and what we would have to go through before we understood. I could not sleep that night.

We left the next morning, taking with us the books and papers that they had given us to read. It happened that at this time my grandniece and two other girls were killed in a fiery accident while driving between Goshen and Elkhart. Because the accident was due to a malfunction in the car it received national attention. On our way home we stopped to attend the funeral near Osceola. In this very sad atmosphere, with our emotions so strained, we couldn't hold back some tears. Some people who knew us must have wondered what special relationship we had with this girl and yet were not sitting with other relatives and people who were close to her.

Back home we shared our grief with a few close friends and then the adjustment began. One day several years later we happened to see a documentary in which a doctor was telling how the homosexual was already marked in the womb and that his brain showed a certain difference. This is what Sem had explained to us, that he felt he was born different, but we had not been ready to understand. Now as our learning and healing progressed, so did our impatience with people, especially church members, who were so very sure their interpretation of the Scriptures was correct and who labeled gay people as sinners. I had to think of the Pharisees long ago, who also were so sure that their interpretation of the Law was correct and they could draw such a sharp line between what was acceptable and unacceptable. Jesus had something to say to them and I felt he had something to say to modern Pharisees as well.

In a year Mabel and Christian moved to Elkhart and Mabel found in her church a small group that was very helpful and supportive. She attended their meetings every Wednesday night and we were invited to spend that time with Christian. This was not only helpful for Mabel but it was such a blessed time for us. We played with him and read to him. I remember that after we read Charlotte's Web together Elsie made a Charlotte's Web quilt. We enjoyed watching Christian plan what should go into it. This weekly contact was so pleasant that we continued it for years — until he was in high school.

MY LIFE FLOWS ON

I was in my late sixties and was approaching retirement. I decided that my seventieth birthday, October 17, 1989, would be a good time to leave the office. We knew what we would do when this time came. We had watched the Greencroft retirement center rise on the eastern edge of town near Goshen College. The complex started with a round building with apartments and an office that opened in 1967 in the southwest part of a 160-acre field. Since then it had steadily grown so that it had four cul-de-sac courts south of the central building and two at the north end of the campus, almost a half mile away near College Avenue. There was also a nursing center, a brand new Senior Center and two newer manors close to the Central Manor, known as Manor II and Manor III. We knew the founders, the spirit and intent of the place, and we liked the facilities. Our special concern was that the waiting list was so very long that we wondered whether we could ever get in.

Then in 1989 came the building of the first two wings of Manor IV and a hundred apartments would open all at once. We couldn't let such an opportunity slip away. I moved up my retirement date to March 31 and we lost no time to make arrangements for a place in Manor IV. I planted rhubarb and an asparagus bed in a garden plot provided at the northeast end. My sister Minnie also took advantage of the new openings at Greencroft. She bought an apartment in Manor IV and was prepared to move in as soon as it was ready for occupancy. We helped her get settled in so far as we were needed. We had agreeable, normal sibling relationships, but she had her own car, joined the College Church and we each comfortably went our own ways.

I knew I did not need to do much by way of ending my work at MMA. Someone would be moved up to take my place. I would work as usual up to the last day. Then I would clear my desk and go home. When I informed the administration of my plans, they told me of a class for retirees provided by Oaklawn Mental Health Center. They said if I was interested in it they would pay my fee.

I was glad to join and appreciated this benefit. It turned out that three of us in the class of about nine were Mennonites, but the others had completely different backgrounds. I enjoyed the discussions about such subjects as finances, let-downs, and new relationships.

On my last morning in the office I got a message that I was to come to the dining room later in the afternoon. There I found the heads of the departments and they were having a little farewell party for me. They served refreshments, but I don't remember what they were. It was an informal gathering and the different people had kind words to say. The one compliment that has meant so much to through all these many years came from the young John Liechty who said I was a worker who lived by the practical wisdom outlined in the book of James.

The next month we got a phone call from Mabel's mother, Florence Amstutz. The doctor was now gone, but we and Florence had become good friends. She told us that her friend Edna Bachman was leaving her apartment in Oak Court at the south end of campus that we might like. Edna and some of her friends wanted to move to Manor IV to be closer to the Senior Center and other activities, but Florence thought we might like Oak Court better. We immediately went to see it and agreed that we liked that location. We found it easy to make the change in plans with Greencroft and I quickly planted a new asparagus bed and rhubarb in the south garden plot, leaving my other one for whoever wanted it.

We told our children of our plans and asked them to come home at the same time so that they could choose what household items they would like to have that we were not taking with us. A date was set for as soon as possible after Miriam's school term was over and we had at least one full day that we could all be together again. The Lapp family arrived as did Sem and his partner John Easton, but Biff did not come with Beth for that marriage did not hold. (He came alone several other times!) Beth came with Ruth and her husband Robin Weder. Ruth had met him in Philadelphia and they were married at an Eash reunion, "when we were together anyway!" It was an emotional time for us, and Beth and Ruth especially were moved to see the home of their childhood slipping away.

The children chose what they wanted. When on several occasions two or three of them wanted the same item Elsie thought of a way to solve the problem. She put a monetary value on the items and in the balancing act the choosing was easier and everyone was satisfied. After they left the house seemed so empty and quiet. Only a few things were left for disposal, like the high chair and baby bed which we gave to the Hispanic church. Our small group from church came with a truck that one of them owned and moved us to our new home. The whole transplanting process had gone very well.

We had planned to put our property up for sale and then learned that one of Elsie's students wanted to buy it. We were agreed and set a date for the closing. Just at the very last minute the student backed out, a real upset to our plans. The painter at Greencroft happened to hear us talking about this when we were there and he said he himself would like to buy our place, so that process went smoothly after all.

Oak Court was the second one built when the Central Manor was being outgrown. Of the four courts at the south end of the campus it was located next to Maple Court, which was the westernmost of the four. Oak Court had eight buildings around a large, oval, cement drive with a young oak tree planted at the center. There were carports in front of the eight entrances with visitor parking around the oak tree.

Entering our building, there were doors leading to the four apartments. The Summer sisters, Ethel and Luella, lived in the front apartment on the right side. Their windows looked out on the court and they didn't miss a thing going on there. Across the hall in the other front apartment lived Elmer Stoltzfus, a wise old Mennonite bishop from Ohio—also an excellent cook, as we learned later. In the apartment behind him lived a pleasant woman who moved away before we got to know her very well. Donald and Doris Jantzi moved into that unit and we became good friends. They were our age and we had much in common. They joined East Goshen Church and we learned that he too had been the director of a retirement home in Archbold, Ohio.

Our apartment was in the southwest corner of the building. Although we had such close neighbors, as soon as we closed our door we found we had real privacy and quiet. We had two bedrooms and a bathroom that contained the laundry machines. The kitchen had once been separated from the living room with some kind of artificial partition, but we wanted it removed so that we had room to extend the kitchen table as far as necessary when we had company. When we looked out of our windows to the south and west we could see a considerable expanse of lawn leading out to the garden plots along 15th Street. To the south we could see our own cozy little back yard which extended from the flower bed along our patio to the dense flowering hedge that screened us from the industrial park beyond. We had a quiet location, broken only on summer evenings when the windows were open and we could hear a pounding noise beyond the hedge somewhere. We liked our new setting very much.

We were busy immediately, not only in getting settled, but also tending our garden. Some of the vegetables were ready for harvest and the excess put away for the winter. Since we had no basement in our unit our freezer was lined up with others in a row in the Maple Court basement. I also had to put my loom in Maple Court, storing it at first in a big room at the foot of the stairs. Later I learned of a little hobby room tucked away in the southeast corner. A man now deceased had used it to make grandfather clocks. When it was offered to me I was glad to take it, but before I could set up my loom I had to spend many hours scraping off the floor the hardened drippings of the finish he used on his clocks. I soon was busier than I had expected, yet I planned to weave at least an hour every afternoon because it was so relaxing.

Our church life went on as usual. We shopped at the same stores as before and our interest in programs at the College continued as well. We had no problems in getting to know Greencroft. Some of our friends had moved in before we did, and various social affairs soon got us acquainted with our Oak Court neighbors. Every Friday a volunteer would drop off a green sheet of paper making announcements and outlining the activities and programs coming up. We went to all the meetings, especially those affecting the residents. We liked the monthly Round Table discussions led by our young director, Gene Yoder. He had begun with Greencroft when it was in a little hotel in Elkhart and he continued to be the heart of it as it grew. He would explain what was going on behind the scenes and would draw questions from us residents. He made us feel we were a responsible part of a good, progressive project.

But the activity that helped me most in getting acquainted with Greencroft was to deliver campus mail. Soon after we arrived Esther Graber of our court asked me whether I would consider taking her place. Some volunteer went around the campus with a little cart to pick up all kinds of messages being sent to a resident or office on campus. Another volunteer sorted out the stacks that needed to be delivered to residents in the courts and left them at Central Manor. Twice a week—on Tuesday and Friday—I would pick up this stack and take it home to sort it and plan my delivery route. It did not take me long to learn where people lived and where the offices were. I liked that job.

We hadn't lived in Greencroft more than about a month when the woman in charge of Manor IV nominated me and I was elected to a committee that served as a kind of liaison between the board of directors and the residents. One member represented the board and I represented the residents. In between were the heads of the administrative offices and those in charge of different buildings such as Manor II or Health Care. The director, Gene Yoder, his assistant Rick Stiffney, and the financial controller, Bob Gibson, took the lead and would challenge the rest of us with their ideas for Greencroft. We discussed all kinds of ideas: for instance, should Greencroft provide a nursery for employees? That idea was eventually dropped because it seemed too few mothers would use it. Should we erect another building for Health Care, one that would be independent of HUD? What about an Alzheimer's unit? Was Manor IV filling up so fast that we must build the other two wings soon? Perhaps a maintenance man might be brought in as we discussed some problem about the grounds. We would eventually decide which proposals should be dropped and which should be passed on to the board of directors. I enjoyed this committee which met once a month.

Toward the end of my three-year term I joined an advisory

committee for the new Senior Center. The Center was intended to be available to seniors in the community as well as serving residents. We had periodic Senior Weeks when outsiders were especially encouraged to come and get acquainted with our facilities and programs. We had a lively community representative on the committee who always had comments to make about every suggestion. Basic regulations, like the rule against alcohol, were determined elsewhere, but the director, Irene Koop, and her coworkers would make decisions and appointments for the public's use for weddings, banquets, reunions, or any catering services. Every fall we helped put on a huge rummage sale which we called September Fest. College students often came to pick up bargains.

Elsie's schedule was also full during these years. She continued to visit our "Grandma Hartzler" as well as her former college classmate in the iron lung, both in Greencroft Health Care. She soon saw others there that needed visits and attention. The chaplain recognized her skills and asked her to be part of the "Caring Friends" volunteer group that he was organizing. She found herself getting so involved that she was spending a part of almost every day in Health Care.

On top of this she continued to carry the load of activities she had grown into in other ways. Our church was reaching out to the Spanish-speaking immigrants who were becoming more numerous every month. She was teaching English as a second language and was already so actively involved through the church that she was known as someone to call when a new need arose. She was still helping in hospice at the hospital and was on the board of directors for the Walnut Hill Daycare Center. The Center had suffered a fire and when she heard that the children now had to lie on the bare floor for their naps she gathered materials and called the women of Oak Court to a "frolic" in the Oak Court basement to knot small comforters for Walnut Hill. These would normally be used as covers, but now they also could be pads on the floor at nap time. The need for these little comforters—at Walnut Hill and elsewhere—kept growing so that Elsie kept making them over the years. The tiny pieces not otherwise useful she sewed into strips for my rug loom.

Another example of Elsie's response to a need was her interaction with several Chinese college girls. She saw three of them in a grocery store with their heads close together trying to interpret a price tag. Naturally she asked, "May I help you?" When she saw that they wanted to buy tomatoes she told them not to, that she could give them some from our garden. They were delighted to accept, and continued to enjoy produce from our garden all summer. Elsie invited them to dinner several times and took them to places like Goodwill where they enjoyed spending time. As she introduced them to things American a friendship developed that lasted long after they returned to China.

Busy as we were, we kept in good touch with our children. Location made it easier to be in contact with the Lapp family and we saw each other several times per quarter. Our own family did not try to get together for holidays, for that was when Miriam was unusually busy hosting the Lapp clan. When Miriam and Steve took over the family farm it was still the center for their get-togethers. The numbers increased as families do until she might have as many as forty people for dinner. Fortunately, a niece who recognized the burden promoted making it more of a cooperative affair.

Our daughters in Philadelphia continued to come home once or twice a year. Even in our Oak Court apartment we had room to accommodate the three — Beth, Ruth, and Robin. We had a chance to get better acquainted with him when early in their marriage we spent a pleasant time together in a mountainous area in central Pennsylvania. Miriam and two of her daughters were also with us as we drove to this nature retreat. I remember how surprised we were to see so many dead deer along the highway. We speculated that the road, which still seemed quite new and was not heavily traveled, had not yet taught the animals of the state forest the dangers of speeding cars. We enjoyed the relaxing days in that cabin, staying for most of a week. The scenery was breathtaking. It was spring and the leaves had just come out on the trees. We thoroughly enjoyed the nature trails. One day when Robin was hiking alone he found a lady's slipper. I was so pleased when he took the rest of us to see it. I had never before, or since, seen such a rare flower. Robin was a self-employed handyman who did a lot of remodeling for them and for others. When we made our first trips to Philadelphia he was still around, but that marriage didn't work out either. When our children suffered pain we suffered too, as parents do.

These years our trips east were not devoted to sightseeing: we concentrated on family. Our itinerary was always indefinite. Sometimes we would stop in with the Lapps or the Eashes coming or going—it depended what suited best. At first we quite often stayed with Beth, for she had bought a house. At first she worked in an osteopathic hospital, but after it went bankrupt she found work in a Catholic hospital. We would all eat together as much as we could. Elsie of course would help with the cooking. I found I could be helpful in the yards. At home I had started rooting some grape vines which I now planted in Beth's yard. There was plenty to do in Ruth's yard—I would clear away brush, pull weeds, and cut long grass with a tool especially ill-suited for the purpose, since I had no mower. The girls had found a book they wanted Elsie to read to us, and so we spent several evenings reading together like the days of their childhood.

Our visits would extend for about a week. They took us to see where they worked. Ruth was still working for *The Other Side* magazine and I could help with the mailings. One Sunday happened to be Mother's Day and we had a picnic in the park where others were also picnicking. A roving reporter came around and asked us a lot of questions. Imagine our surprise when we found out we were featured in a piece in the *Philadelphia Inquirer*!

On Sundays we naturally went to church with our daughters. They attended the historic Germantown Mennonite Church, the first Mennonite church in America. We saw the first little pioneer building. It was too small and antiquated to be used and the congregation was renting space in a hall. The membership was somewhere between fifty and one hundred. They were struggling to get along as best they could, for they had been removed from the roll of their conservative district conference because they welcomed gays. Nor was there any kind of support from the conservative sister congregations around them. They were determined to be an "open church" for everyone, free from the rigid regulations of the mother organization. I was not used to their informal urban ways and did not feel at home with them and yet I admired their courage and their efforts to stay a Mennonite church, though with liberal ideas. Their former advisor or "shepherd" from the conference was sympathetic enough that he stayed in contact unofficially. Their pastor had his own struggle to get along financially. He had some apartments to rent and once when we arrived he offered us an empty one for the week.

I had heard from some source that old age was divided into three parts. Those between 65 and 75 were the Young-Old-Aged who were still active and busy. The Middle-Old-Aged (75-85) were losing energy and ambition and were threatened by infirmities. The Really-Old were over 85. I saw myself slipping out of the Young oldies into a Middler who had less energy to get things done, yet didn't want to be idle and completely retired. I found there was still plenty to do.

For example, the old metal shed at the south end of the campus had blown down and Greencroft had built a neat little tool shed to replace it. By now there were more and more gardeners so that it was already too small. Greencroft was willing to replace it, but I proposed that we gardeners erect a toolshed ourselves so that we could have it sooner. Fellows like Paul Troyer, Perry Miller and others agreed to the plan so that Wes Zook, the groundskeeper at the time, was willing to gather materials and head the project. After taking measurements from the old shed in about a month we had a neat twin building standing beside it and everyone was satisfied.

A year or so later we had a similar experience—those of us who liked to do shop projects found that the Homan building was getting too crowded. Again I suggested that we shop workers put up an expansion. I called it the barn and I went every day to work on it and to coordinate the efforts of the others who came to help. Again within a month we had made more room to everyone's satisfaction.

In these years when computers were becoming more and more available and popular I became very curious about what they could do. Then I read an article that described WebTV which could do many things a computer could, but was less expensive and less complicated. That appealed to me and when I saw an ad for one I couldn't resist buying it, although I had no keyboard. I was able to get one of those at Wal-Mart and the maintenance men hooked it up for me. A neighbor who also had WebTV helped me with a few introductory suggestions, like how to find Yahoo. I enjoyed playing with it, constantly learning new things until I was even able to make my own birthday cards. I was having fun, but I was tying up the telephone line and the more frequent calls for Elsie could not come in. Naturally this caused some tension which I resolved by watching when Elsie would leave the house for her visits and then hustling to the WebTV!

My sister Minnie was definitely showing her age and her health was slipping. I had taken over the care of her car and I prepared her taxes. She was driving less and less and I began to take her to the store every week. She could ride the church bus on Sundays. Before long she would simply hand me her grocery list. We always took her along if we were going to the same place.

We no longer drove to Kouts twice a year to see my sisters. Lydia died in 1980 at the age of 68. Bessie was now the only sister left at Kouts; Mary lived in Michigan City. Carrie had lost her husband Alvin and now in these later years married Amos Hostetler, a widowed minister who lived in Emma, a tiny village in adjoining LaGrange County. That was much closer and we had so much in common that we began to be back and forth about every six weeks. Whether we had dinner at our house or theirs we always had Minnie with us.

During these years Henry and Esther Yoder (Elsie's sister) moved from Grantsville, Maryland, to Goshen because their children were living in the area. Since there was no opening at Greencroft they took temporary housing nearby. We were all so pleased when after several years an apartment became available across the court from us. Naturally we were back and forth often. Both sisters were busy with outside interests and concerns, but we often ate at each other's homes and we attended the same church. Each Monday evening Esther would cook for as many of their family as could come. Their son Roger was a pilot for American Airlines, flying in and out of Chicago.

We were seeing more of Sem again. Perhaps he had felt like delaying a bit until he could be surer of our understanding and acceptance. One Mother's Day he sent lilac bushes which the maintenance men planted along our hedge. We enjoyed those lilacs a lot as long as we lived there. Of course we were invited to Sem's graduation when he received his PhD in history from the University of Chicago in 1982. We rode the South Shore train to the city where he and John met us at the station in their neighborhood. Mabel and Christian had driven up and so had her twin sister Mary and her husband, Glen Gilbert. We sat with the four of them and John at the ceremony. The thing I remember best about the whole thing was how the undergraduates threw their black mortarboards up in the air as far as they could fling them after it was all over. Afterwards we stood around on the greens during all the personal congratulations and farewells. I enjoyed watching little Christian walk around wearing his father's maroon-colored doctoral tam. We all had a supper together at Sem and John's place before leaving for home. Elsie and I could ride back to Goshen with the Gilberts.

We had much more contact after Sem and John bought a cottage along Lake Michigan on the Michigan side. The cottage was really a double house and they bought it jointly with a Chicago friend, Linda. It was such a good place to get out of the city, where they could relax, swim, and enjoy nature. Linda had considerable remodeling done on her side, and Sem and John had also done some on their side. After our first visit there, Sem told us where we could find the key and told us we could come and use the cottage whenever it was empty. The invitation also extended to the rest of the family. When the Lapps brought along more friends than could be comfortable in the space on their side they were welcome to spill over into Linda's side, and she had the same privilege.

Elsie and I went alone to the cottage several times. It was located on a street that was parallel to the shore of Lake Michigan. We would follow a path about a block long through woods to a set of wooden steps that led down to a landing from which another set went down to the beach. We liked walking along the water, collecting shells, and going as far as the lookout at the public beach. We also enjoyed the woods so much and the many birds. We took our girls to the cottage several times, and twice we were all there together as a family. That was a special emotional time for Elsie and me.

In the very beginning it was hard for Elsie not to blame John for breaking up Sem's marriage, but that feeling didn't last long as we learned to know John. He was an agreeable fellow, tall like Sem. He enjoyed making pots as a hobby and had a kiln at the cottage. Every Labor Day he would display his pottery at the roadside and he could easily pick up a thousand dollars each time.

At this "middle stage" of aging we had to face the infirmities that went with it. Elsie had noticed when she was still teaching in the schoolroom that there seemed to be some arthritis in her knees. It was not serious and she paid no attention to it. When our children were gone she and I began to take long walks. At first we walked along the railroad tracks towards the College. Now we were walking regularly around the court circles at Greencroft. Each year Elsie had always fallen once or twice, but she would always scramble to her feet and go on. Her pain kept increasing until she needed to consult a doctor. At first he removed worn-out cartilage and gave her shots, but the time soon came when he said she needed replacements.

She decided to have both knees replaced at once, even though she knew that the pain of the process would be doubled. The operation was successful and because I was retired and available, I was trained to give her the recovery exercises so that we could take her home and avoid the expense of the usual rehab. We dutifully went through the fifty stretches every day but before we were finished her pain was almost too much to endure. Then she discovered that the exercises were to be taken through the day and not all at once! Church people brought in ample meals. I could divide the leftovers for other meals, putting them in the freezer if necessary. I would barely be started washing the dishes before she would call me for help to get into a better position to endure the pain. I would return to the dishwasher for only a short time before she was calling again for help to try a different position for relief. It was quite an ordeal for both of us, but after six weeks she felt so much better than she had for years. Even so we bought her a motorized chair and soon she was resuming her visits and ministries, as peppy as ever.

The magazine that Ruth worked for, *The Other Side*, eventually folded, but she had already gone to work for Peter Buttenweiser, a philanthropist whose family were among the heirs of the Lehman Brothers financial firm. Her boss was a passionate Democrat and in 2004 when Evan Bayh from Indiana was running for a second term in the Senate, Peter invited forty or so of his rich friends to a fundraiser for him. When he found out from Ruth how her parents had supported Evan's father, Senator Birch Bayh, back in Indiana, he invited us to come to the fundraiser dinner as his guests. He paid our airfare, our hotel expenses, and furnished a limousine to take us wherever we needed to go! The tables for the affair each seated eight people and of course we were seated with Ruth. In his introduction Mr. Buttenweiser told of how much Ruth had been helping him and after his tribute to her he asked her parents to stand: the only representatives from Indiana and good supporters of the Bayhs. What a heady experience it all was for us!

Since we knew that Elsie's nephew Roger Yoder would be flying into Chicago we chose a flight home as close as possible to his so that we could ride back to Goshen with him in his car. We easily found each other at the airport, but were shocked by the message he had just received. His father Henry had died that morning. We knew that Henry had not been up to par ever since he had his pacemaker inserted, but his death was a real shock to us all. He had died in his sleep. We therefore came home greatly subdued.

After we had been at Greencroft for about ten years I began to notice a few little pains in my chest and sometimes I was a little more out of breath than usual when I delivered the campus mail. I didn't pay much attention to those warnings for they had not been very frequent or very strong. Then on one hot summer day when I was making my rounds the symptoms were so much stronger that I knew I must do something about it. I went to Dr. Paul Yoder who had an office on the campus. He recognized the trouble at once and promptly sent me to Dr. Mark Smucker, the heart specialist, who surprised me by putting me in the hospital immediately to have my blocked arteries catheterized. He intended to insert stents, but discovered he had the wrong size. He kept me in the hospital until the right size could come from Chicago. There was nothing for me to do but wait and watch television.

As I came home my main instruction was not to overdo. I could do some weaving, some gardening, driving locally — in other words, I could live quite normally provided I did not exert myself too much. I could no longer carry the mail or drive on long trips. Unfortunately, after three months scar tissue had developed and I began to show the same old symptoms as severe as before. Now it was clear that I needed bypass surgery. Neighbors and church people drove me to South Bend for these necessary appointments. Miriam and Steve came to be with us and to sit with Elsie during my operation. I can't remember whether I had a 3-way or a 4-way bypass. When I asked the doctor later, he couldn't remember either.

I made a satisfactory recovery. After two or three weeks I returned to Greencroft Health Care and Elsie could see me every day. In fact at first, away from the hospital, I felt panicky if she was not there. There was an empty bed in my room and I was so relieved when I got permission for Elsie to sleep there for two nights until I felt better. When I could come home there were rehabilitation exercises at the Roman Gingerich Fitness Center at the College. We had to be there at six in the morning. This was not our choice, but had to be scheduled that way because of an arrangement between the hospital and the College. A nurse would take my blood pressure and then we would walk around and she would take it again. We kept increasing the rounds until at six weeks I could consider myself practically well.

Now in these later years when we went to see our daughters in Philadelphia we went by train and Ruth would meet us at the station in her van. They too had been through health misfortunes. Ruth had been diagnosed with ovarian cancer. Now when she needed help Beth was on hand to tend to her needs. We were so relieved to hear that she was responding well to her treatments, but the doctor warned that they could not remove all the cancer; she was to be aware of her limitations and have regular checkups. Although she was doing well, we worried that she was not obeying her admonition well enough, for she was going on as though she was completely well.

Then it was Beth's health that was deteriorating. Her rheumatoid arthritis was giving her more and more pain. The space in the backbone for her spinal cord was getting narrower and causing increasing pain. She had several surgeries to slow the process, but it was becoming very difficult for her to sit. When they came to see us Ruth had a seat in the van readjusted so that Beth could lie down as they traveled.

Meanwhile, since both were living alone, they decided to move together. They bought a three-story house and Beth moved into the first floor. Ruth's living quarters were on the second floor and she was reserving the top floor as an office where she kept her computer and other equipment. We could foresee the time when Beth would have to move to the second floor and require still more of Ruth's care.

On these later trips we saw more of Philadelphia. Ruth took us to see museums and other points of interest. I was impressed with the farmers' market—so large, so many booths, and such a great variety of things to sell. When we found out that we were living near the oldest continuously operating funeral home in America, Elsie and I walked over to see it. A friendly attendant took us inside and showed us everything that was open to the public.

A location I was especially glad to see was the American Friends Service Committee, the Quaker peace office. Our own Mennonite office was in Akron, Pennsylvania, but along with the Church of the Brethren the three denominations were all part of NSBRO, the National Service Board for Religious Objectors, in Washington during World War II. In front of this Quaker building was a historical marker erected by the Pennsylvania Historical and Museum Commission. It read:

> During World War II, some 12,000 men who were classified as conscientious objectors to war - about fifteen percent of them from Pennsylvania - served in non-military occupations across the United States. Under the leadership of the Mennonite, Quaker, and Church of the Brethren agencies, they were engaged in mental health

care and medical experiments, in forestry and on dairy farms, and in other important civic projects.

We took pictures with the sign and then they took one of me alone beside it. Ruth put that one into a frame and they placed it near my chair in our apartment. I can no longer see it, but it symbolizes for me the satisfaction that we fellows had made a significant contribution in a peaceful way.

One Sunday morning we drove to church with a dish for a carry-in dinner being held after the service. I dropped Elsie off at the entrance and went to park the car. She was chatting with the greeters at the door and then turned to see whether I was remembering to bring her casserole from the car. Somehow she lost her balance and fell hard on the cement. She could tell at once that she was seriously hurt. One of the greeters happened to be a trained ambulance assistant. He and a nurse who was nearby took over. In a short time the ambulance had arrived and I found myself riding with Elsie to the hospital. I never did find out who took care of my car or that casserole!

Elsie's hip was indeed broken and she had surgery yet that day. The bone was very hard. We found out she had Paget's disease, a bone disease in which calcium is not absorbed as it should be. In another day or two Mabel came to see Elsie. With a doctor's eye, she noticed that Elsie's foot was turned out in an abnormal position. The surgeon admitted he was aware of that, but he felt he could not keep her under anesthesia any longer in order to fix it. In another day or two she had a second operation. She recovered well from both surgeries and in about ten days she was moved to Greencroft's health care unit. There she was well taken care of and in about three weeks she could come home. Meanwhile I had been eating with Real Meals at the Senior Center. Now we received Meals on Wheels and I could use the leftovers for our suppers.

Now I began to do more of the housework on a regular basis, like running the sweeper and doing the dishes. I was now past 85, one of the Really-Olds. Except for the church I held no regular jobs outside the home. I had time to repair and putter and help around the house as well as play with my computer besides doing some weaving and a slowed-down version of gardening. I was taking more interest in cooking and paid special attention when Boyd Nelson brought over an unusually delicious loaf of bread he had baked himself. I wanted to know more about that and learned that he had a bread-making machine. As he told me about it, I knew I would like to try that myself. I bought one of those machines and tried out the recipes he gave me. Then I read that Mary Ann Lienhart-Cross, a home extension educator out of Purdue, was conducting a class in bread-making at the county fairgrounds. I promptly enrolled and found the session lasting from 10:00 to 2:00 to be interesting and helpful. As one would expect, our noon lunch featured different kinds of breads.

I had been having regular checkups for my teeth and eyes, as people usually do. I knew my eyes were changing, but I didn't realize how much until one day I saw that the cracks in the sidewalk did not stay straight, but zigzagged in unusual ways. This required attention. The local optometrist said I had macular degeneration, but it was the dry kind. The process was going so slowly that I could go on reading with a magnifying glass, could see the TV fairly well, and I could still enjoy using the computer.

After about two years the doctor said the bleeding had started and now I had the wet kind of degeneration. He sent me to Dr. Grossnickle, a specialist in Warsaw, who said I needed laser treatments, but instead of administering them himself he preferred that I go to a specialist in South Bend who did nothing but laser work. My close neighbors, Charley Neff and Jack Hubbard, took turns getting me to my appointments. After six treatments the bleeding stopped, but my eyesight was no better. I was declared legally blind. They gave me a letter officially stating this which I could show as necessary in taking the next steps.

Legally blind! This was an unexpected blow. As I looked into my future as a blind man I realized it meant that I could no longer read, weave, drive, or take measurements of any kind. I would find it awkward to eat or to meet people. I would not be able to see the faces of my grandchildren. How my life would change! I had to think about Longfellow's poem about a rainy day in the fall of the year. After describing the scene he shifts to the dreary, "rainy day" experiences that can come into a person's life. He ends the poem, however, on this note:

> Be still, sad heart, and cease repining;
> Behind the clouds is the sun still shining;
> Thy fate is the common fate of all,
> Into each life some rain must fall.

I had always been one to accept what I could not change. That stood me in good stead now at this point in my life. After all, my little world would not crash if I was blind. I still had peripheral vision. I could still hear, walk and talk, dress myself, and go places. I could use an electric razor. I simply had to learn to do things differently.

It also occurred to me that I could have a good umbrella for this rainy part of my life. ADEC, the Association for the Disabled of Elkhart County, was an organization formed to help people with various disabilities and impairments to become as independent as possible. They had a department just for macular degeneration. A representative came to Greencroft every other month to help people like me. At these meetings I would have opportunities to consult with her. She arranged for me to get talking books and a talking watch. She sent assistants on house calls to advise people regarding their specific needs. They could put raised markings on the stove burners and provide such things as wide-lined paper and pens that wrote a wider, plainer script. ADEC could also tell us when and where to use our official letters.

There were also individuals who kindly stepped in to help out. I called them my ministering angels. Several people volunteered to read to me. Son-in-law Steve took over my taxes. It was hard to give up my loom, but I was so glad that my granddaughter Rachel Lapp showed an interest in weaving and wanted it—the loom could stay in the family. Esther brought us our church mail and special church information. She would also check to see if we needed anything from the store. Her daughter Kathy Hollsopple became our local power-of-attorney and came to help us with health management. Our children would take note and provide anything they happened to see that might add to our convenience. I also appreciated those many unnamed or unknown "angels" who might do a kindness on the spur of the moment, like helping with a door, or holding my umbrella, shielding me from any little mishap that might have occurred, or helping at the dining table.

Then there was Elsie, the greatest angel of all, the best of the best, who years ago accepted me and stayed loyally by my side no matter what loomed before us. She would do the driving, write the checks, read the newspapers or Sunday School lesson, and attend to so many details beyond all number.

And so, dear family and friends, as I look back over my life I am reminded of the words of Tennyson's Ulysses:

> I am a part of all that I have met;
> Yet all experience is an arch wherethrough
> Gleams that untravelled world, whose margin fades
> For ever and for ever....

Elsie and I, in faith, will go through that arch together into that unknown world.

[Elsie Eash Sutter died on June 28, 2010.]

October, 2003

Days may not be fair always,
That's when I'll be there always.
Not for just an hour,
Not for just a day,
Not for just a year,
But always.

"Always," Irving Berlin, 1925

Index of names

(The numerous references to Clayton Sutter and Elsie Eash Sutter are not indexed.)

Miller, Jeptha, 43

Miller, Joseph D., 43

Miller, Katie (Miller), 43

Miller, Lewis, 41

Miller, Lizzie (see Reinhardt, Lizzie)

Miller, Luella (Miller), 41, 64

Miller, Lydia (Egli), 43

Miller, Maria (Mast), 42

Miller, Mary (Hochstetler, Eash), 64-65

Miller, Nancy (Yoder), 43

Miller, Perry, 137

Miller, Roy, 43

Miller, Samuel B., 41, 43, 64-66, 73

Miller, Tobias, 43

Miller, Yost, 43

Mishler, Dorothea, 42

Nafziger, Bernice, 1

Nafziger, Carroll, 1

Nafziger, Chris, 1-2

Nafziger, Dan, 10-11

Nafziger, Nellie (Miller), 1-2, 42, 64

Nafziger, Victor, 1

Neff, Charles, 146

Nelson, Boyd, 145

Oyer, Bessie (Sutter), 14, 16, 25, 27, 57, 138

Peters, Abe, 111

Porter, Gene Stratton, 108

Pratt, Grace, 17

Pratt, Lyle, 17

Raid, Howard, 122

Reinhardt, John, 18-20, 25, 65, 73

Reinhardt, Lizzie (Miller), 18, 22, 41, 45, 60, 66, 73

Reinhardt, Stella, 27

Riley, James Whitcomb, 108

Risner, Rachel (Lapp), 146

Roosevelt, Franklin D., 56, 75, 92

Rost, Dr., 1

Schantz, Edna, 124

Schertz family, 13

Schwanke, Lilah, 79, 81, 83

Shetler, Sanford, 90

Smucker, Dr. Mark, 117, 141

Springer, Ben, 10

Made in the USA
Lexington, KY
18 June 2013